:9

9

Canoe Design and Construction

Also by Alan Byde

BEGINNER'S GUIDE TO CANOEING
LIVING CANOEING
CANOE BUILDING IN GRP

Alan Byde

Canoe Design and
Construction

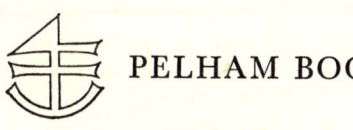 PELHAM BOOKS

First published in Great Britain by
Pelham Books Ltd
52 Bedford Square
London, WC1
1975

ISBN 0 7207 0862 1

Set and printed in Great Britain by
Tonbridge Printers Ltd, Peach Hall Works, Tonbridge, Kent
in Baskerville eleven on twelve point on paper supplied by
P. F. Bingham Ltd, and bound by Dorstel Press, Harlow, Essex

Contents

Introduction

If you want to know how to make a canoe, start reading at page 91 and work towards the ends of the book from there. If you want to follow the logical sequence from the conception of the idea to the launching of the finished boat, start at the beginning and work right through it. If you want to know how to handle a canoe, don't read this book; but if you want to know why a boat behaves as it does, then this book may help you to analyse the craft.

The method used is simple. The ways in which one can put a set of lines on to paper are many and various. Several books on yacht design will help you to develop more sophisticated ways to draw the design of a canoe. Frank Goodman who criticised the book for me would like to see the use of buttock lines. He is a canoe designer. Agreed, they are useful, but in this case not essential. Regard this book as a first step in design and drawing.

'If it were necessary to know everything before attempting anything, then nothing would ever be done.' So said my father, Alf Byde. I think it is the most liberating concept I ever had given to me. It is the reason why I think I can help you to design your own canoe. There is more to it than that. The British Canoe Union gave me the title, 'Senior Coach' way back in 1961, and the Award of Merit followed in 1966. In the simplest terms that represents a great many miles of water under my keel.

What is it that starts one designing? I did some thinking on this question for this book, and arrived at a vague impression, when I was four maybe, which was in 1932. There was a comic (was it *Chick's Own*?) and a picture of a red and yellow speedboat surging through the blue water of a bay surrounded by white cliffs, yellow sands, green hills and people playing in the sea. It was captained by an outrageous chicken with a red hat and fatuous grin, his little mate had a blue hat. The speedboat

I remember, it was short and wide and deep, with a whaleback foredeck and a steering wheel. On what slight pins do large doors hinge.

Bill Saunders and Bill Cramond started me off building canoes in 1957. Bill Saunders said 'Simplificate and add lightness' and invited me to consider the converse. Courtenay Phillips, who criticised this book, shuddered at this gross misuse of the English language. In fact I have had a battle with myself to retain it. But I defy him ever to forget it. I can't. That misuse of the language is completely at variance with another idea which I felt has helped me, and the man who taught me carpentry, Bert Smurthwaite, gave it to me. 'If it looks right, it is right.'

These are the things which have helped me to design canoes. Now that word, 'canoe' is often misused in Britain. The Americans have the better way, and use the words kayak and canoe in their proper places. However, such is modern development that white water 'Canadians' look very much like kayaks. Perhaps we could all agree on a compendium word to describe the floating devices we now use. How about 'Canak'? Who was that who said 'Kaynoe'? Is it utterly impossible to get it right? So long as there is uncertainty, then designers can flourish. The beauty of boats for me is the opportunity one has to achieve simplicity in line and function. If ever Armageddon comes, there won't be any wheels left.

CHAPTER ONE

Design Origins

Boat design has for a long time been a matter of evolution rather than revolution. Then came plastics, and the whole basis of building changed. Here is a thought. 'Why does a boat have pointed ends?'

What is a boat? The name is a universal sound. Bateau, boot, barqua. Before highways were built, the waterways offered just about the only means by which heavy and bulky objects could be moved. Design was based on natural material and the ways in which it was possible to work them.

Around Britain boats are still being built to ancient designs, designs which are not written down, but like folk songs, are carried in the builders heads; like the distance between this piece and that piece is a forearm's length plus a hand's breadth ... the plugs are as long as my hammer shaft ... and so on. Coracles are built in Wales and on the Severn in England. Curraghs are built up and down the coast of western Ireland. Cobles are built along the north-east coast from Flamborough to Bamburgh.

> *Old joke:* 'A bench fitter works to the nearest thousandth of an inch. A loco fitter (steam) works to the nearest inch. A shipwright works to the nearest ship.'

The reason that boats have sharp ends is that when you take planks of wood and pull them into a boat shape, the ends of the planks meet in a naturally pointed end. There is no regulation which states that all boats must have sharp ends.

To ask the right question is to be half way to obtaining the right answer. Your first question about the design of any boat is, what do I want it to do? Then you will think perhaps ... but if I don't use it for that all the time what other thing can I use it for? Maybe you use the boat and find yourself

9

involved in some other water activity that is nearly but not quite what your boat can do. So the boat is modified. I have a coracle from Carmarthen which is a Towy fishing coracle. I have seen a coracle which is a Towy sprint coracle. You would have some difficulty in handling a lively 20-lb. salmon in the sprint coracle, or in racing over a hundred yards at Cilgerran each August in a fishing coracle.

Noah was told to build an ark. He put animals in it. One supposes the fishes managed for themselves. How large does one make a pen for a rhinoceros, sometimes known as the wealthiest animal in the zoo? How does one dispose of the manure, or store the fodder for thousands of creatures? Noah had no books to tell him, or at least I don't think he did. Yet we have a very clear idea of what an ark looks like, probably inspired by toymakers, our design foundations.

Did you ever watch a seagull on a rough patch of water in a fishing harbour, or off a breakwater nearby? It is moved this way and that and as a consequence of its movement you can read the wave currents that cause it to do that. A full size fishing boat would be in serious difficulties just there at that time. A kayak might very well behave more like a seagull than a fishing boat at that time and place.

The kayak is a very neat piece of compromise. How can you make a useful boat shape with less than five long pieces of wood to make its keel, chines, and gunwales? Three pieces, maybe, but then you have difficulties with either excessive beam, or lack of stability. Trees simply do not grow tall in cold latitudes, so long timbers are at a premium.

The great fighting ships of Britain and Holland, Spain and France, had gun walls. The designers of these ships worked from very detailed drawings. From these descended the great clipper ships, built to carry cargo, people, wool, tea (etc.) all over the world; to compete and beat other ships to the world's markets and so get the best prices for commodities. The sails they carried have names to stir the imagination; Mainsail, topsail, lower topgallant, upper topgallant, lower royal, upper royal, skysail, and even moonsail. The ideas that conjures up! Ghosting along on a quiet night with every stitch on her, orders to take in sail, and men scattered on a yard seemingly nearer to the moon than the deck. Romantic blarney? I don't know but I think that these shapes, lines, and ideas have become embedded in my mind and will in due course express their power in some probably untraceable way.

These ships behaved in different ways. Built into them were subtleties which made for speed off the wind or into it; a wet ship in a blow, and in a storm the sea looting the deck of all kinds of gear and goods; or a dry ship riding the stern seas in safety. Some gave their passengers a rough ride, and some were the essence of comfort. Yet all these ships were intended to do much the same sort of work. The designers tried all manner of ideas, so many compromises. Make the spars heavier and she can carry more sail; but that implies stronger standing rigging and that needs a hull to take the thrust of rigging and mast butt. Compromise, that is what all designers must do. A canoe designer will sacrifice stability for speed, but a good designer will make his craft just as fast, and retain a little more stability.

A designer carries a heavy responsibility. He offers a kayak design to people who want some sort of boat, and because this

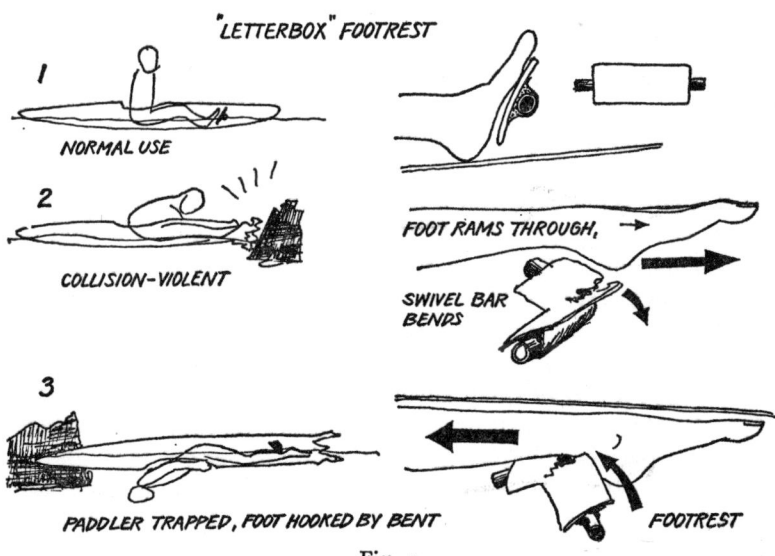

'LETTERBOX' FOOTREST

1 NORMAL USE

2 COLLISION-VIOLENT

3 PADDLER TRAPPED, FOOT HOOKED BY BENT

FOOT RAMS THROUGH,

SWIVEL BAR BENDS

FOOTREST

Fig. 1

kayak is offered the customer buys it trusting that it will do the work required of it. He later finds (say) that it carries a lot of windage, and he is blown about the sea, unable to control it, is carried on to rocks and lost. Not long ago a footrest system was used by many canoe builders, which seemed to be satisfactory, simple to install and cheap enough. It is quite probable that at least three young men died because this type of footrest failed 'dangerous'. Now we use a type which 'fails safe'.

Recently, at the College where I am employed, the students took part in the National finals of the Surf Lifesaving Association. In this event there is a surf ski event for single skis. It is a race from shore, around a buoy, and back across a line on shore. Distance about half a mile, or possibly up to a mile. It involves a journey out through the breaking surf, and then a ride back through it.

A surf ski is a sort of surf board which could be used to rescue someone else, it is like a long malibu board, flat bottomed, rockered, and the paddler sits on top, using kayak paddles to propel himself. A good size wave and he is wiped off the board. I argued that the design could be changed as most of the time is spent in displacing water, not in planing. Therefore a displacement hull will win. Plug the paddler into the deck in a cockpit and he cannot be wiped off. In fact, use a kayak design, a rounded vee bottom not flat, and pointed ends not barge type as in many surf boards. We did this despite many doubts. The students said quite rightly that they were expected to win in this thing, and was I *sure* I was right? I answered, 'No, but at this late stage have you a better alternative, and lets find out, shall we?' They did try and they came in second in a field of eleven of whom five were wiped out in the break going out. The verdict : 'Wow!' 'A *great* boat.'

Once I ran a canoeing centre in Oxford. I had bright ideas and spent time and money developing the ideas. One was a surf 'shoe', a sort of small kayak with a surf board bottom, built for planing on a surf wave. Some shoes already in existence were turned over backwards when trying to get out through the surf, because for planing performance one must have the paddler's weight well back, and that implied not much boat behind the paddler and lots in front, so that when he went out through the wave he fell over backwards, apex over base. Balance requirements prevented lengthening the boat at the back. Speed requirements prevented widening it too much, apart from which to make a boat wide spoils the paddler's paddling action. The only other dimension in which one could extend the boat was upwards in the rear deck. So I did that.

When you take a boat of given length and width and raise its rear deck you inevitably get a slab-sided effect. Well, we built the boat. One only. It must have cost about £25 for materials for the plug, £15 for the mould, and £12 for the boat. Time cost was probably well over 200 hours. Club members took part. Making it took some of the steam out of making other boats which we could use on the river. What did it cost? Probably 15–20 useful canoes is one way of expressing it.

In use the boat went out through the break in fine style. No reverse loops. Then came the ride in. Because of the big slab side at the rear behind the centre of lateral pressure, there was a vane effect in the broken wave, and the BAT Mk 7, for such it was, went sideways, do what we could. That is not permissible with a surfing boat. No stylish waltzing about the wave face, just a grim ride, broached. To what extent was I justified in taking other peoples money and assuming I could bring forth a new design for them to use? I did, however. I offer the idea that the designer should also be confident and not over-awed by the possibility of failure.

An Australian living in Surrey, Pete Smith, wrote to me at the beginning of the year and asked if I could recommend a suitable load-carrying kayak for a journey to Australia. Sounds easy enough when you say it quickly. Intended route London, Thames, Dover, Calais, canals of France, Germany, Danube, Black Sea, across Arabia, the Euphrates, Persian Gulf, shores of Pakistan, India, Malaysia, and so to Singapore and then by boat to Darwin.

He arrived on the shores of the Black Sea just before Christmas, was arrested by the military as a suspected spy . . . well what would you think if some chap in a kayak came cruising along carrying a shot gun, a revolver, a short wave transmitter (SARBE), a transistor radio receiver, and a compressed air harpoon gun? Look for the numbers 007 I suppose.

The kayak he is using is a copy of an Aleutian baidarka, the original of which is to be seen illustrated in *The Bark Canoes and the Skin Boats of North America.* I was able to pick up the essential lines from the small, $3\frac{1}{2}$-in. long drawing, and make a working set of lines from it. This was turned into a plug and a set of moulds and the kayak made was the third to be produced. The fourth kayak hull taken from it made the basis for the surf ski that I have already described.

When he came to build his boat, that which has taken him across Europe, he had little time and no knowledge of how the boat handled, but he trusted my confidence in this untried kayak. Apart from the fact that it weathercocks (always points into the wind), the boat has done well. The weathercocking was cured with a rudder which is in any event an advantage on a long journey like this.

The questions that one asks, and are asked of one as a designer come oddly and by chance; the replies that are found equally so.

CHAPTER TWO

Compromises

Designing a hull requires a fairly certain knowledge of what that hull must do. In small hulls, as small as canoes and kayaks, there is a long history of development, but very little is laid out in a formal way, such as the standard aerofoil shapes which are used in designing aircraft. Therefore we should make educated guesses, with one eye looking back at the past, and the other watching where modern material can take us.

Speed-weight
Some qualities of a boat are quite incompatible. To illustrate that remark by reducing to absurdity, let us accept that a light-weight craft is better for racing, as it accelerates more rapidly, sits higher on the water and thus causes less drag, and so on. Let us reduce its weight to zero. The canoe then ceases to exist, but it would accelerate very well if it did.

There is also the point to be made that the paddler's weight is an indispensable part of the assembly. As canoe weight becomes less, the law of diminishing returns applies, and so to lose 5 lb. from a 35-lb. boat might be helpful to an ace competitor, to lose 1 lb. from a 25-lb. boat would be of little advantage compared with the sacrifices of strength that would of necessity be required. To reduce the weight to 18 lb. as has been done requires perfection in building ability and perfection in materials, and as a result the cost rises dramatically.

A long kayak will go faster than a short kayak, other things being equal. The increase in speed is approximately proportional to the square root of the increase in length. If a hull length is doubled, then the speed increases by 1.414. Say the hull was 10 ft. long, and its speed was 4 knots, then the speed of the 20-ft. long boat should be 5.656 knots, all other things being equal. To double the speed of the hull, its length must be multiplied by a factor of four. Therefore to go at ten times the speed, the hull length should be multiplied by a factor of one hundred. Imagine a hull one thousand feet long? Its weight would be very great if it were to be strong enough to keep that length in the water, *i.e.* to resist bending under the load of its paddler. To spread the loading equally along its length would require very complicated structures. In a thousand metre sprint the paddler would be about two-thirteenths of the way to the finishing line at the start. In any event the International Canoe Federation Rules would disqualify the freak before it was launched. The longest single kayak I ever heard of is a 26-ft. long kayak used for hunting caribou in Canada. Clearly there is a length at which the solo paddler can obtain useful speed without losing too much in other ways. Effectively it is between 12 and 20 ft.

Manoeuvrability-speed

The sport of slalom requires a manoeuvrable kayak or canoe. Rules specify minimum length and maximum beam. Let us suppose that rules were not specified. Then make a canoe just as wide as it is long, in fact a coracle. That can be made to turn in any direction at the slightest flick of the paddle. But such is the nature of the flow of water around the hull, that the hull has no 'sense of direction' it doesn't have a back or front and so it doesn't point any particular way. Steering a coracle requires an understanding of vectors and relative velocities. I don't suppose the Teifi fisherman would describe the way he paddles his coracle in those terms, but see the way he moves it about the water.

Because the hull is short, about 4–5 ft. long, and about as wide, its speed is very slow, about 2–3 knots. To compete against other kayaks that would be moving from gate to gate pretty quickly would require a paddler who could plane the thing all the way around the course, still cleaning the gates with skill and accuracy . . . some problem that with the gate width only 4 feet. Man-powered planing hulls are about the equivalent to man-powered flight, it is possible for very brief periods, but its not likely to happen in the normal run of things. On the other hand we could make a kayak which would get from gate to gate very quickly, say a K1, speed about 7 knots; trouble there is the approach to the gates would be so swift that it would not be possible to line up a gate with finesse. And turning the thing would be so slow that the average paddler would be halfway down the course before he got halfway round. There is an optimum size for that sport, and it is about $13\frac{1}{2}$ ft. by 24 in.

Structural weight

Given that we accept optimum lengths and beams for different purposes then let us try to reduce the weight of the boat as much as is possible. This too is governed in kayak racing. The builder of the boat may decide to use carbon fibres to give his hull a lattice work stiffening, and so allow him to reduce the glass laminate thickness, say from a specific weight of three ounces per square foot, down to one ounce per square foot. One would say, reduce it from a 3-oz. hull to a 1-oz. hull. The trouble is, the carbon fibres will cost a very great amount, and only a highly skilled laminator could so handle the glass and resin and the carbon strands in order to get the last ounce of weight out of the structure. In use the hull is rigid and light, but very quickly there is stress cracking in the thin glass laminate around the edges of the carbon fibre stiffening. Such a boat may survive only a few runs in heavy water, before requiring repairs, and they add weight. Such a boat would be about four times as expensive as an ordinary one, and it would have a short life in service. But for a short time it might be worthwhile for an ace slalom paddler, or sprinter to use one. But then a sprinter would use a moulded-wood boat anyway, which costs about five times what a glass boat costs. One may consider when designing (amongst so many other things) whether carbon fibre will be used in this structure, and if so, is it really worth it? For a given use and shape, there is an optimum weight for the hull which allows minimum weight with maximum possible strength; and that depends on having first-class laminators who can get the best out of the resin and glass; in fact a knowledge of the various qualities of glass and resin will affect this decision.

Structural weight, Aleut Kayak

Since writing the piece on the Aleut (*see page* 13), I have seen

Peter at the Canoeing Conference at Crystal Palace, an annual event. He was 'persuaded' to leave Bulgaria as his presence on the Black Sea at a time when no tourists were about apparently embarrassed the authorities. He put his kayak on show, plus all his equipment. He made a very telling point to me.

It was this, when the kayak is carrying a vast weight, easily four or five times its own weight, it is impossible to lift it, so it is more usual to drag it. This when done over rough ground causes lots of nasty cracking noises in the hull. When one's intention is to continue to Australia, these noises are very worrying.

Because normal portaging by carrying is not possible, light structural weight becomes unimportant. In fact it is better to build a much heavier canoe than usual. Instead of building to a 3 or $4\frac{1}{2}$-oz. specific weight, a 6-oz. hull with a $4\frac{1}{2}$-oz. deck would be more in order. The shell is then much more like a dinghy for thickness and strength.

When Peter sets out again he will be in Aleut 11 mark two, and it will probably weigh 70 lb. unladen, instead of the first boat's 40 lb. A wheeled trolley is not on, as it is too easy to break, in addition the gadget is difficult to store on board. We are thinking now in terms of a kayak sledge as used by eskimo seal hunters on ice. This sledge may have runners, or it may simply be a thick shell which clips over the bottom of the hull where this rubs along the ground. The shield will carry a pair of strong stainless steel runners glassed into its thickness.

Rotational inertia

Let us consider another aspect of canoe design. The double kayak illustrates it better. To obtain better paddling it is a good idea to have the paddlers at least six feet apart. Then the fore paddler does not hinder the aft paddler and vice-versa. Perhaps this kayak is to be used in 'heavy water', that is, maybe it will often be rough where this boat is used. A wet boat at sea is a chilling thing, and a dry boat will always give the crew a better ride. After a half hour of constant soaking in waves, you long for warmth and dryness. Apart from which you get salt in your eyes, you cannot see very well, and it hurts.

The kayak may be twenty feet long. If the paddlers are 6 ft.

apart, and they are centrally placed for weight in the kayak, then they are each 7 ft. from the ends. When one end lifts to a wave, the other end goes down. When a mass changes its place, it must accelerate. You start getting into considerations of rotational inertia and all kinds of higher school mathematics. Flywheels are often used to illustrate this effect. It is that when you put weight further out on a rocking beam, it rocks more slowly, and when you bring the weight (or, properly, mass) closer to the pivot point it rocks more quickly. The effect on a two-seat kayak when the paddlers are well separated is to slow down the rate at which the hull rises to a given wave. The closer together they are, the more rapidly the bow rises to a head wave. A white water racing Canadian two seater has the paddlers close together, overlapping even. This is possible because they are using single-ended paddles. The slalom Canadian has the paddlers far apart, but this is for quite a different reason, so that they can get accurate turning, and for this they can sacrifice a dry boat. A seagoing kayak must be a dry boat, so the paddlers should be as close together as they can be ... but then you get the front paddler scooping up pints of water on each stroke and dropping it on the lap of the chap behind, so he gets wet anyway. There is an optimum spacing to be found.

Weight carrying/windage

Suppose you require a weight-carrying boat, something that will contain anything up to 100 lb. of equipment. The simple thing to do is to make the whole thing slightly bigger, increasing the length, beam, and depth. Maybe you have a good hull, of fixed length and beam, but you could increase its bulk by increasing overall height. You add a strip, say $1\frac{1}{2}$ in. deep, all around the gunwale line, and then you attach the deck to that to make the new plug. It works. Heavily loaded, it performs much as before. But lightly loaded, it rides high. There is a lot of boat above the water surface. On a river this would not be of much account. On the sea where the wind always blows, there is a noticeable effect. It has a lot of windage. Some canoes or kayaks are built higher in the first place, in order to make them more stable, for example, without having a wide beam at the waterline. In that way one obtains speed and stability, but only at the cost of extra windage. Again, one obtains some characteristic, but only at the loss of efficiency in some other way.

Speed/waterline beam

Each boat has an overall width, or beam. This is naturally measured at the widest point. Each boat, for a given load, will also have a waterline beam in a similar way. When a hull tilts over, it has a natural inclination to return to its original position, but when it reaches the point of no return, it capsizes. If the hull can be arranged to have a high free-board all around, then as the boat tilts over further and further, more and more of the hull side sits on the water, and so the ability to return to its normal level condition continues. There are some natural limiting conditions for example when the cockpit becomes tight under the armpits, or when windage becomes too great a problem.

Weight/strength (See also Appendix 3)

Perhaps you want to build a surfing canoe or kayak. Really this is a builder's problem, but design can be affected by this requirement. In grp, (glass reinforced plastic), the heavier one builds the boat, the stronger it becomes, Surfing puts heavy demands on the craft, and the crushing power of a big wave (which may be from 8 to 16 ft. high) when it breaks is very great. The canoe can suddenly be subjected to external pressures which vary from 3 psi over atmospheric (15 psi) to atmospheric, all in a split second.

It is in the nature of surfing beaches to be gently sloping, and so as the tide goes out, large tracts of sand are exposed, and the canoe on the car roof may be half a mile from the water's edge. So you hump the heavily-built canoe on to your shoulder, and you walk half a mile to where the action is. On the way there, the wind (which as you know always blows on the sea) swings the canoe about like a weathercock. The bite of the cockpit rim into the shoulder muscles becomes noticeable. You pray for a lighter boat. Now if you get your shape right, you can actually balance the lower gunwale on the hip, with the shoulder inside the cockpit rim. You can provide the inside of the cockpit rim just forward of the seat side, about where the thighs press, with a smoothly rounded rim which is comfortable to grip, and to ease the weight of the canoe on the shoulder by pressing upwards with the hand. If, by some oddity of design, you have the point of balance of the canoe just where the seat sides are, then keeping the thing on your shoulder will be difficult, as it will continually wish to slide off your shoulder. It is much better to have the shoulder bearing upward inside the cockpit rim immediately in front of the seat side, and again the rim must be designed to be comfortable, both for the thigh and for the shoulder. It has occurred to me to make a small yoke, just for one shoulder, so as to spread the load, and thus ease the bruising effect of the rim on the shoulder.

Class rules/handling qualities

Suppose you have a slalom kayak. It is built to go round a slalom course as quickly as possible, and must manoeuvre easily. One way to avoid clipping the gates as they hang there, supposing one's handling ability is limited, is to make the line of the bow and stern decks run down almost to the waterline. In this way a high hanging gate, or even a normally hanging one, may be avoided simply by slipping under it. But this has penalties. As the canoe enters a stopper wave, or turbulent water, because there is a low deck fore and aft, there is little resistance to water coming over the ends. There is little tendency to rise over the water, but a decided tendency to plunge through. In this way the boat becomes really wet, and may get into difficulties in heavy waves, simply because it is not big enough at the ends to derive the necessary lift from what buoyancy it does have in order to generate the vertical acceleration to keep the paddler above water.

To avoid the difficulty to some extent, you can give the deck a steep pitch, like a house roof. The idea is that the water will run off, as down a steep hill. But this must lower the gunwale line, and so, to obtain a given beam, the hull must be flat bottomed and shallow. This makes it sticky in the water, because of the increased surface area under water, and the point of no return in a capsize is soon reached. This makes demands on the handling skill of the paddler. The tendency now is towards deep hulls, and flattened decks, and increased handling ability. There is of course the point that a higher gunwale line makes for extra stability, and allows a narrower waterline beam, thus making for more speed. But the deck line is higher and so low hanging gates must be cleaned by skill and not boat design.

Critical speed/rocker

This is the speed at which the boat changes from a displacement hull to a planing hull. For a given length the boat will have a certain critical speed for a given load. The loading has

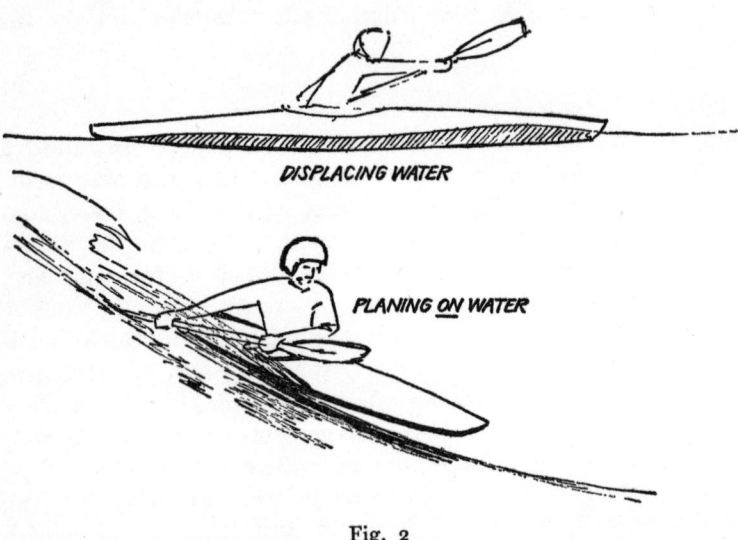

DISPLACING WATER

PLANING ON WATER

Fig. 2

little effect on this speed. As man-powered planing is like man-powered flight, it is rarely experienced. Shall we say that the critical speed for a given boat is 6 knots. Up to 4 knots it will be easily paddled. Up to 5 knots it will require some extra effort, but not a great deal. 5½ knots and one is working hard to keep it there, and 6 knots just won't come. The increase in effort is enormous, the bow lifts, the stern squats, the bow wave is the full length of the hull and the next crest of the bow wave is interfering with the crest of the stern wave. Once planing at over 6 knots it all becomes much easier.

Suppose that one requires a manoeuvrable hull, then there must be a great deal of rocker on it. At rest this boat may have just the same waterline length as a boat built more for speed, which has almost no rocker. All other factors are assumed to be equal, except that the rocker is different. As the highly rockered hull is pushed along, it tends to rise in the water at the bows. This is largely a function of the rocker deflecting water downwards instead of cleaving it aside. As soon as the bow rises, which it does easily because the stern doesn't have much buoyancy to resist the downward thrust at that end, the waterline shortens quite rapidly, thus increasing the planing tendency, and so the critical speed for this hull is reached much more rapidly than that of the hull without rocker, which will continue to keep its full waterline in the water right up to the moment it reaches its critical speed.

If one could keep the nose down on the highly rockered boat, that would help. So you can have a cockpit which is well forward of the centre of buoyancy. However, this makes the stern very buoyant, and the canoe becomes nose heavy whilst manoeuvring. The boat weathercocks most horribly, and entering a gate it tends to slew out at the stern, hanging out the stern it is called, thus clipping gates.

Directional stability/manoeuvrability

Most novices when paddling tend to wander about. In a group of ten you will always find one who meanders about at the back of the group, repeatedly ramming the bank, and getting frustrated going nowhere. Another will show every sign of considerable ability, and the other eight will vary between the two extremes. Now if one has a hull which is directionally stable, this tendency is reduced, and so the group makes better progress. It is possible to make a hull directionally stable by giving it a slight vee bottom, a fair amount of 'dig' at the back and front. However, one then goes on to teaching them how to turn the thing, this it resists, and you have lots of people trying hard to turn it without much success. Going sideways becomes much more difficult too.

There are various gadgets which can be fitted to a hull which turns easily. You can fit a detachable skeg, which is taken off as the novice gains skill and can control the boat. Or you can fit a rudder which has moving parts which get bent or fall off, especially when the boat is not a personal boat. You may even have such a wealth of resources that you can put novices in directionally stable boats at first and transfer them to manoeuvrable boats later.

The racing paddler reading this will be unimpressed, as in this field the practice is to put the novice straight into a racing boat which is very stable directionally, but there the compromise has been with lateral stability, and so the novice falls gently over whilst travelling in a straight line. Theory is he soon gets used to the balance of the boat and rapidly enjoys the sheer speed of the craft.

In sea going, a directionally stable boat is a good thing, but in choppy conditions, where the wave length is about boat length, the effect the wave currents have on the hull is very pronounced, and much energy is needed to turn the boat. On balance I would prefer a directionally stable boat on the sea.

Style/building problems

One of the most beautiful sea-going kayaks is the Anas Acuta, modelled on a native eskimo kayak, in fact very like the Greenland kayak from Disko Bay, 1882. (*Bark Canoes and Skin Boats of N. America*). It has very noticeable raised bow and stern lines, with pronounced sheer towards the ends. It makes a very pretty boat and a dry one in the sea. However, in order to join the hull to the deck when building it, one needs a very skilful laminator. He must have very good equipment and a steady strong hand to support the very long pole needed to guide the brush over the joint. There is in fact a stunt one can use to shorten the length needed to be joined by nearly 15 in. on this boat. A canoe builder in the north-east has copied this design and he has reduced the overall length and taken off the strong sheer at the ends. This makes it much less difficult to join, but it has also turned out to be a very wet boat at sea, a rather undesirable quality.

A point to be considered when designing a cockpit is whether to make it large or small? At sea, a large cockpit enables one to root about looking for kit needed en route, but when in heavy breaking waves, a large spray deck tends to burst inwards under pressure rather more easily than a smaller spray deck. An expert kayak handler will probably go for a small cockpit, and keep his day tackle on deck, whilst a less confident person may prefer a large cockpit opening which is easier to get out of.

When designing a boat for speed, one usually gives it a sharp bow and stern so that it cleaves and closes the water easily when close to its critical speed. However, when laminating this sharp end, the laminator must get his brush right into a limited space. Experienced laminators can do this, but novices cannot. The result of inexpert laminating in this case, is a rough bow and stern line caused by bubbles in the laminate breaking through. When designing, one should know who are the people likely to build the actual boat.

Strengthening ribs/stress concentration

It has been the practice for some time to build canoes a little lighter, and to stiffen this lightweight laminate by glassing in stiffening ribs. Longitudinal ribs along the line of the keel or the deck ridge, are quite normal and present no serious difficulties. Transverse ribs do present difficulties. In addition, if one makes a bulkhead, so as to provide an air tank buoyancy system, then where this cross bulkhead is glassed to the hull there is considerable local rigidity.

What happens on impact with a rock, is that the hull flexes inwards along the line of the point of contact with the rock as the hull continues to slide along and over it. If it reaches a strong and rigid point on the hull, the hull cannot simply bend away from the obstacle and then spring back, so it tends to crack along the edge of the stiffener. After a number of impacts at this point, the hull splits along the line of the bulkhead or stiffener. I call it stress concentration.

There was a practice of building the deck very light, say one ounce, (specific weight) and stiffening it with six or eight herring bone stiffeners both fore and aft. This was fine, but quite soon the constant flexing of the deck causes stress concentration around the edges of the stiffeners, and the deck split into sections or panels.

Some materials are very tough, such being a polyester woven material, called Diolen. In this case stiffeners are not needed, but the cost is high and the skill needed to make it is also rare. Not only that, if the canoe should literally wrap itself around a rock, one's legs may be trapped which in a normal grp hull would probably result in the hull ripping away from the deck allowing one to get out, but in a polyester fabric hull would result in one being trapped, perhaps fatally. It is necessary to put a grp deck on to a polyester hull so as to minimise this problem.

CHAPTER THREE

Restrictions on Design

There are many forms of restrictions on your design. Basically I list them as follows.

1. Who wants it.
2. Where is it to go.
3. What is it to be made of.
4. When is it wanted.
5. How much can you spend.

1. Who

It may be wanted by a competitor for competition purposes. In these international days when this book will probably be read all over the world, to specify British rules would be wasteful. In Britain, write to the British Canoe Union, 70 Brompton Road, London SW3 1DT. Otherwise you should contact your National sporting body for racing rules. Many of these specify a class and minimum beam, minimum weight, and maximum length, particularly *where* length is measured. For example a rudder could be said to be the hinged rear part of the hull; and if the rudder isn't included in measurement but you so streamline the after hinged part that it behaves like part of the hull, you have a longer and potentially much faster craft. The experts spotted that one long ago, so you cannot 'cheat' under the rules now. Similarly one could give the hull sides a hollow flare so that the minimum beam rules were satisfied, but the waterline beam was much less than that. Its been done, and thrown out. Concave lines on Competition K boat hulls in any case are not permitted.

You may be designing for heavy men with heavy equipment who are intending to travel by sea to remote places and to live out of their kayaks for a week or two. The design will be very special then. Or you may be designing for youth club or school children to make their own canoes, and to use them on local quiet rivers and canals, just for pottering about. School time-tables have an influence here, because you cannot go far be-tween break and lunch, or in an afternoon, if Mum will be waiting for junior at 4 p.m., so long fast kayaks to cover long distances which are not easy to make won't be much use. Short manoeuvrable canoes like BATs might be just the thing.

2. Where

Well, the permutations are endless. Let us suppose that you are designing for just one type of person, about 170 lb. weight, and not stuck for time, a keen adult clubman. Does he want to go on white water rivers? (One indication of this is, does the river fall at least fifty feet in a mile? In stages, of course. Long flat stretches on what should be rough rivers, are to be regarded with grave suspicion, as they presage a sudden drop.) Maybe the canoe is to go on lakes. Maybe what is wanted is a short kayak for surf, or a long sea-going kayak for sea journeys rather than surf gymnastics. Maybe the newly introduced types of surf-ski are required, mainly for lifesaving patrol off busy beaches, or for competition in National events in these classes. One group intends soon to go to the North Cape of Norway, and will be paddling the Nordkapp kayak, especially designed for this expedition.

3. What

There are many ways of making floating objects. Apparently, in the Himalayas, on the upper reaches of some rivers, inflated goatskin bags are used to float across fast rivers. Boats are made of grass, and once I saw a rather horribly shaped but none-theless working 'kayak' made from rolled up newspapers proofed with varnish. *The Times Educational Supplement* had this on its front page, about 1965. Floating devices can be made from blocks of polystyrene. A friend of mine at Southampton was given a block 4 ft. by 8 ft. by 1 ft. thick. They lashed on to it a transom of plywood, to which they clamped a small out-board and four of them went adventuring in the creeks off Southampton Water. They have been involved in the floating bicycle, which wins races across muddy creeks being quite the fastest way from point 'A' to point 'B' when a small item like a river lies in the way without benefit of a bridge.

Canvas on stringers and frames; plywood sheets stitched together by wire and sealed with glass tape and resin, as developed by Ken Littledyke; thin plywood panels joined by butt straps, and then sheathed in glass and resin as developed by Ron Vardy; D. J. Davis designed a kayak from two sheets of marine plywood cunningly cut and tailored and joined, but simple to make and very quick; cold moulded veneers stapled and glued together . . . all these methods have been well illustrated and detailed.

Last summer we took some blocks of polyurethane foam, and some plywood. The outline was cut in plywood, both for plan and profile, full size, and then the foam was glued into place between the panels. It was sawn roughly to shape with a carpenter's hand saw, smoothed with glasspaper, odd holes stuffed with slips of the foam, and the whole sheathed in glass cloth and resin. We had a competition double surf-ski in about four days. The surface was poor, but it did prove a point. It wasn't cheap to buy the foam, but the plywood was second hand, and the glass and resin was cheap enough. It weighed rather a lot, and took in water which caused it to become too heavy. It will make the plug for the grp model which will be turned out in due course. Some surf-ski enthusiasts in Cornwall use polystyrene foam with a single central stringer and they sheathe it with glass cloth and epoxy resin, which does not attack the foam as the more common polyester resin does.

The description of the polyurethane method may seem a bit long winded in this context, but it leads into the next section.

4. When

When is this wanted? For me the quickest way to introduce an original design is to use the polyurethane block method, using cut-out frame sections to check the shape from time to time as it is sanded down, and sheathe in glass and resin. You can then use the prototype, and alter it to suit your needs, or to correct faults as you find them. When the model satisfies you take it and work on it with filler and polish to make a good plug, and turn out grp moulds to make production craft in the course of time.

If time is not so important, then you can produce a plug and set of moulds if you put in about 20 hours of concentrated work a week (spare time) and it should take you six or seven weeks to produce the plug, moulds, and first canoe, using the method described in the book. That has the disadvantage of not allowing you to try out the prototype before making the first production moulds. In that case I always regard these as pre-production moulds. I hardly ever get it right first time. The BAT mark 5 took three different plugs before the final one, and that spread over ten months before the first boats were on the water and performing satisfactorily.

Just about the most tedious method of building I used was to make a jig from rough timbers, and then to staple and glue strips of veneer to each other over the jig. That took about a year and a half from start to finish, and I did lose interest a number of times and had to restart; but the final boat was strong even if it did fall over every time it turned sharply. It was called Byde's Persian Slipper, and ruder names by those whom it upended.

One group of Scouts at Oxford had just finished, after two years of labour, their first grp canoe mould when I arrived next door with three moulds to choose from and an open invitation to use them. I can quite understand their reluctance to put aside their own carefully done but rather lumpish canoes, the product of so much loving care and hard work.

5. How

How much can you spend. At present prices (January 1975) at the College we charge students £25 per grp canoe, for the materials and use of mould and workshop. People outside the College we charge £30. £25 is barely enough. Only two years ago £12 was the top rate. Resin prices have soared during the last fifteen months. I think that £25 is a fairly representative minimum price at present. If you are a Scout group in Britain, you are probably on to a good thing as many manufacturers of resin, or big users of it, will let you have some very cheaply or as a gift. Scouts do definitely have an advantage here. It's worth going begging, for few twelve-year-olds can afford a canoe straight off, and there is plenty to do once you have the material.

You could build in cheap materials, like old tarpaulins from trucks, and using plywood which used to be the lids of cardboard barrels in which sausage meat was delivered. I did this once, and it came apart five years later off Hartlepool on 8 November 1964, a date I shall not forget. Paddling a bag of splintered rotten sausage-barrel lids ashore from half a mile out on a cold lumpish grey November day is not on. Not any more. I think that cost about £6 at the time, although £10–£12 was more usual for canvas covered canoes then.

You may buy or even beg a crushed canoe from a canoe club, something that has been through the stopper for the last time, or surfed ashore full of water and on to rocks ... this old wreck can be stuck together with a sheathing of glass and resin for about a quarter of the cost of building a new one, but it requires some skill and care to get the shape back.

Finally, the last restriction on building your canoe, or better still designing it, is enthusiasm. Given that and a bit of gumption you can cross oceans.

CHAPTER FOUR

Drawing Requirements

I have assembled various odds and ends, and they are as follows.

1. An old drawing table, although any table top will do provided it is flat and without ridges or blemishes.
2. A 2-ft. steel rule.
3. A 6-in. plastic rule.
4. A piece of rubber eraser.
5. Several pencils, mostly 2B.
6. Rotring pen and stencil set. 0.6 mm.
7. Tiny hand stapler.
8. Roll of sticky tape.
9. Piece of medium sandpaper on which to sharpen pencils.
10. Roll of tracing paper.
11. Sheets of drawing paper, squared, $\frac{1}{10}$ in. squares. 20 in. by 30 in.
12. Some sheets of scrap paper.
13. An artist's brush with a fine tip.
14. Bottle of black drawing ink.
15. A black felt-tipped pen.
16. A flexible curve, and a set of French curves. (Not much use, but Frank Goodman tells me that 'yacht curves' are available and are much better, I must have a set!)
17. Some sheets, pieces and strips of thin card.
18. A desk lamp. I have used an 'Anglepoise' for some time, but now I have an adjustable spot light mounted on the ceiling beams. I started off with a table lamp set in front of me, years ago.
19. A clip board with sheets of scrap paper on which to make the notes and calculations whilst sitting by the fire watching TV.

Drawing essential lines (plan, profile)
As in Figure 3, take the squared paper, (1) and draw a line

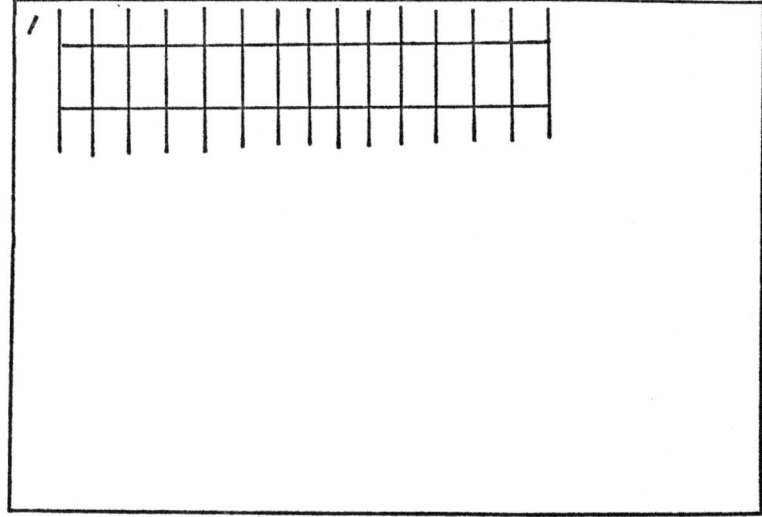

Fig. 3

about two inches below the top edge, on the left hand side of
the sheet. This line is one-tenth as long as the finished canoe is
to be. It should start about two inches from the left edge of
the sheet. Below this line draw another parallel to it and as
long, with three inches between them. Mark off the stations,
with the common interval between them, shall we say, one-
tenth of a foot. You now have a grid, as in the drawing.

Now, bearing in mind the many things already detailed, you
sketch in the profile. Use a soft pencil, lightly. In general the
gunwale line is about two-thirds of the way up the canoe hull
from the base line. The cockpit opening is towards the rear of
the canoe rather than the front. The cockpit opening is about
27 in. long. The centre point of the canoe will be about 3 to 6 in.
in front of the centre part of the cockpit. Look at what you
have drawn; brood on it. Then perhaps you will rub it out,
lightly, and start again. You will get a smooth curve eventually.
A good way to check the accuracy of the curve you are drawing, is to sight along it. Sudden changes of curvature will show
up easily. and you can identify tiny irregularities in the curvature in this way. Pin point the centre of such bulges in the line
by using your finger. (Fig. 4).

B

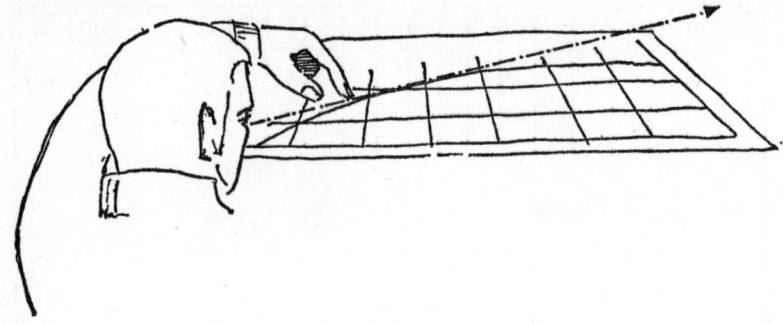

Fig. 4

As soon as you are satisfied with the profile, draw one side of the canoe on the plan. Obtain a true curve, you can use a flexible curve or French curves, but I prefer to work freehand by eye alone. You soon cultivate an eye for a true line, provided you are particular in identifying weak points in the line, and by erasing and re-drawing establish a good line. Clearly the other side of the canoe is a mirror image of the first.

Try to be accurate, but remember that this is a one-tenth scale sketch, and it is used primarily to help you to make up your mind. You will take measurements off this small sketch, scale up ten times, and transfer to another drawing where full scale smoothing of the lines will be done.

Having established the outlines of the canoe on profile and plan, ink in the required line. There will probably be several fine lines out of which you will wish to pick one. Use a curve and a drawing pen and so establish the line. Erase the pencil lines. If these have been done lightly with a soft pencil, then it will be easy. If you have used a hard pencil heavily, then you will have permanent lines on the drawing which may be wrong. If the drawing is by now a little grubby, do not worry, as it will not be required after you have traced the lines on to a properly presented drawing.

The next big and decisive piece of thinking is about the master section. (q.v.) There are so many alternatives possible within the basic lines that many checks and balances must be applied within the mind; the mini-computer of the brain must think, and think hard about this section. The section must be drawn-out full scale on the second piece of squared paper. That process is dealt with in the next section.

Having obtained the waterline beam on the master section, transfer this measurement (reduced to one-tenth) to the one-tenth scale plane. Put the waterline on the profile, parallel to base datum line, at the required depth. The profile waterline will cut the keel line as the rocker rises up to bow and stern. Having found these two points on the profile mark them off on the plan as well, one being exactly above the other on the drawing.

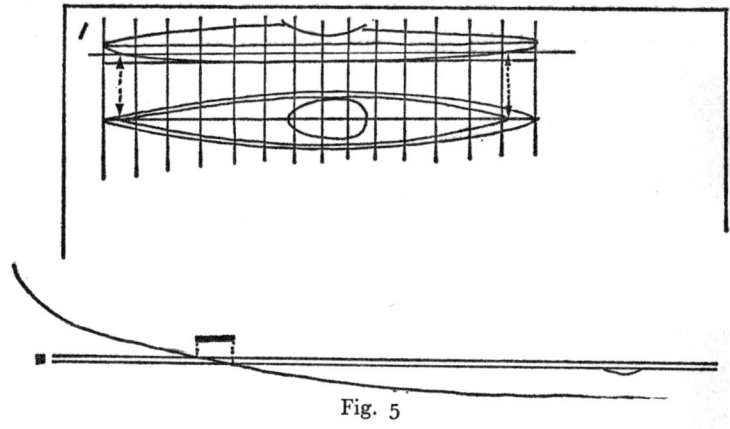

Fig. 5

Now, on the drawing, there will be four points on the plan which show where the waterline will be. Sketch in the required waterline noting that it runs more or less parallel to the gunwale line. The waterline runs within the boundary of the gunwale line in most cases. There is a quality, tumblehome (q.v.), where the hull is wider at the waterline than at the gunwale line. This is often found on Canadian canoes, and some racing kayaks.

Drawing these lines which cross others at a fine angle may involve a small vertical variation which produces a large horizontal variation. The drawing shows how this happens. Be aware of the probability that this will occur, but do not be worried by it. The next stage in drawing should iron out these variations. Remember also that the plug maker must turn your drawing into a shape, as accurately as he can. The slightest slip with a plane or sanding machine will very quickly remove, or put on, a tiny error. If you are to be the plug maker, remember that a shipwright works to the nearest ship. This is no excuse for sloppy work, but is intended to re-assure you that a good boat might not be exactly what the drawings specified. If you were employed by, say, Struer of Denmark, there might be a great deal of pressure upon you to be very accurate in your work.

You should now have on sheet one a grid of pencil lines, plus a clean inked profile and plan showing gunwale and waterlines. On sheet two there will be the full scale outline of the master section, and the next part of the book deals with how to draw this.

Drawing the master section

Take the second sheet of squared paper (Fig. 6), number it '2' in the top left corner. Draw a centre line up the sheet. Draw a line parallel to the bottom of the sheet about 2 in. up from the bottom edge. The two lines meet. This is the basic grid on which the master section is drawn. The height of the

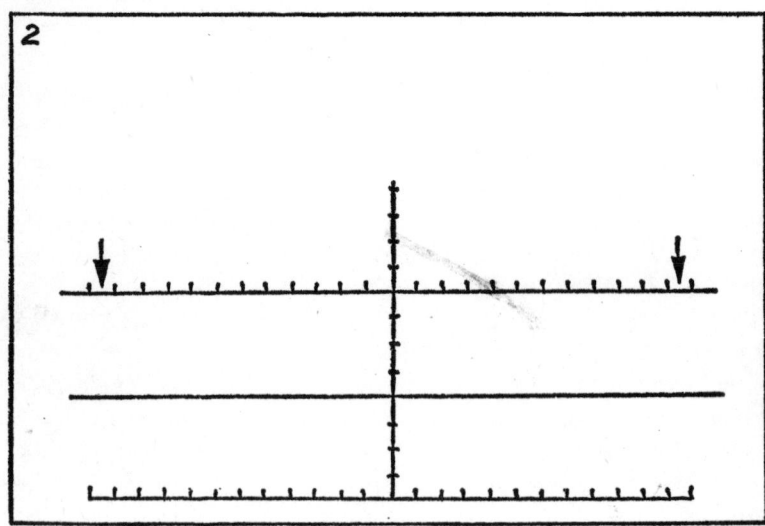

Fig. 6

vertical line is the same as the required depth of the canoe, and the width of the horizontal is the same as the required beam of the boat. Mark off these lines in inches, starting from the point of intersection. 12 in. each way is about right.

Now, using soft pencil, sketch in the outline of one half of the master section. Transfer this outline to the other side of the vertical. Look at the master section outline with great care. This will decide very much how the boat handles. If not satisfied, rub it out and start again. Leave it overnight perhaps, sleep on it, think about it. Do something else for a day or two, then come back and try again. Very often the mind has been working on the problem quite unconsciously, and you can then solve the problem. It is much better to 'waste' time at this stage than to plough on, get it wrong, and commit hours of time to further drawing, followed by ten times as many hours to the building of it.

From this drawing, and the considerations that have gone into making it, it should be possible arbitrarily to decide where the waterline will be. This is the calculation waterline (CWL). I find this usually lies about 4 in. up from the deepest part of the hull. The total depth of the master section will be between 13 in. and 11 in. for a full size boat for an adult, and between 11 in. and 9 in. for a child. The total beam will be about 24 in., perhaps less for a sea-going kayak. A racing kayak will be about $19\frac{1}{2}$ in., but class rules will apply here. The waterline beam may be between 1 and 2 in. less than the maximum beam, but planing hulls and tumblehome will alter this 'rule'.

Figure 7 shows two quite different master sections, but both have the same overall beam, the same waterline beam, and the same depth. That on the left is of a chine hull, that on the right of a round bilge hull. The chine shape is suitable for plywood and canvas boats, the other for grp, or possibly canvas. Some of the thinking which goes into these shapes is as follows.

The round-bottomed hull will be fairly vee-bottomed, as round hulls go, which will make for speed, but will lack ease of turning. It might be suitable for a lighter load, and it will not be suitable for carrying heavy weights. Given the other

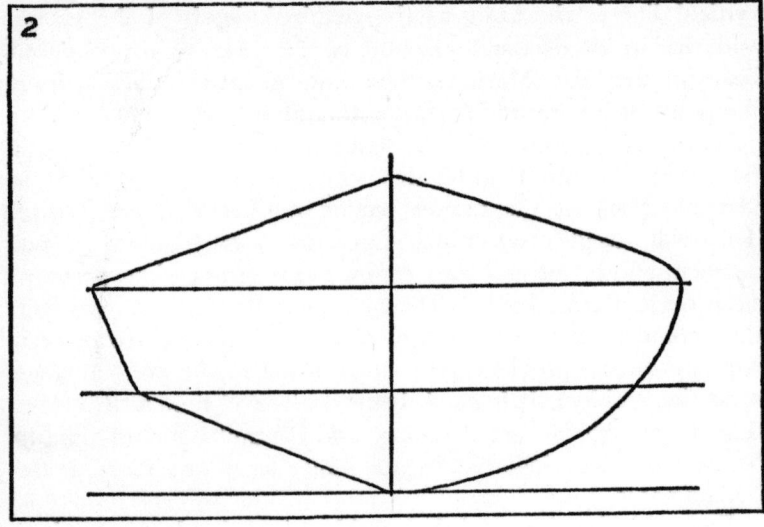

Fig. 7

lines of a sea kayak it will probably produce a sea-kindly boat. (*Sea-kindly: sort of happy on the sea . . . difficulty to describe.*) The hard chine section would be suitable for building in plywood. It will sit deeper in the water for a given load, compared with the round-bottomed section. It will be very directional and will be very slow to turn. In that case it may be decided to give it more rocker, say an inch at each end. However, that will tend to concentrate the buoyancy of the boat at the centre, and so it will tend to sit even deeper. To counteract that, it may be necessary to make the hull more barge-shaped in plan, giving it wider sections at bow and stern. The point is that as in all boat design, an alteration at one point will affect all other parts of the boat, and so the design must proceed with harmony in mind. It improves with practice.

Now, having decided the master section required, ink it in using curves. Make sure it is what you want, for once it is established an echo of its outline will be found in every other section in the boat, with decreasing emphasis as you move away from it, towards one end or the other. After this is done, you may wish to decide bow and stern sections before going to the next part of the drawing. It is not essential at this point. If you do so, then do it as follows.

Start with the bow section. It is usual to show the bow sections on the right of the centre line, stern sections on the left. However, I have done it the opposite way around; there is no special reason for this except lack of training to do it in the accepted way. Whatever the reason the section shapes are not affected.

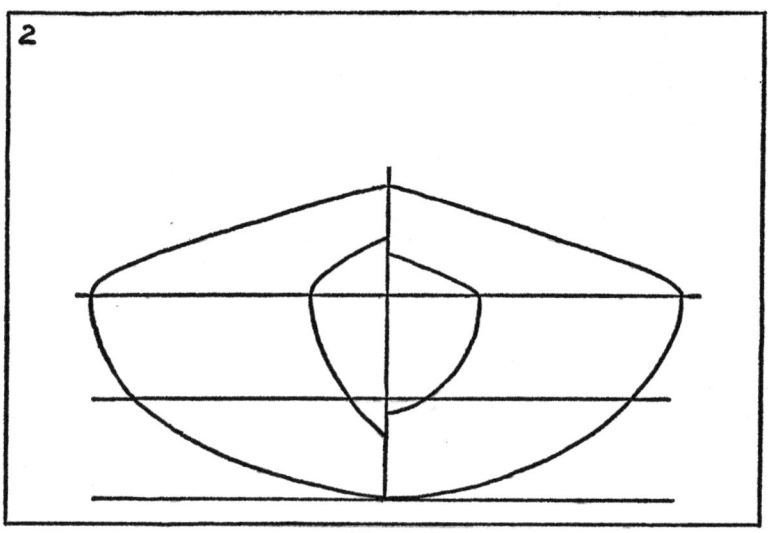

Fig. 8

Take a station one foot back from the bow. Working from the one-tenth scale sketch, take off degree of rocker, deck height, gunwale beam and waterline beam, and transfer these to the master section grid. Link up with a smooth curve. Think about it. The degree of thinking should not be so much as for the master section. In general a river canoe will have a gentle vee-bottom at the bow, with a flat stern section, thus making for a stern turning hull. There is also likely to be less bow rocker on a river canoe, so as to give the bow more dig, or hold in the water, compared with the stern. A sea kayak might have a very deep and narrow vee section at the bow, so as the bow plunges through waves a gently increasing degree of lift is developed by the deep vee shape. This compares with a slamming, or hammering effect of short stubby bows as are found on river canoes, when used at sea.

The stern section is developed in the same way. Take a station one foot fore of the stern, and take off measurements as for the bow section. If a hull is required which is directionally stable, then give it some 'dig', by giving a distinct vee to the bottom line. If the hull is to turn readily, then the bottom shape should be flattened, and appreciably wider than the bow section.

The drawing of the three master sections (Fig. 9) shows how the outline can be different, although each has the same dimensions. The first will be fast, tender (i.e., tip easily) and directional. The second will be slow, turn easily and be a load

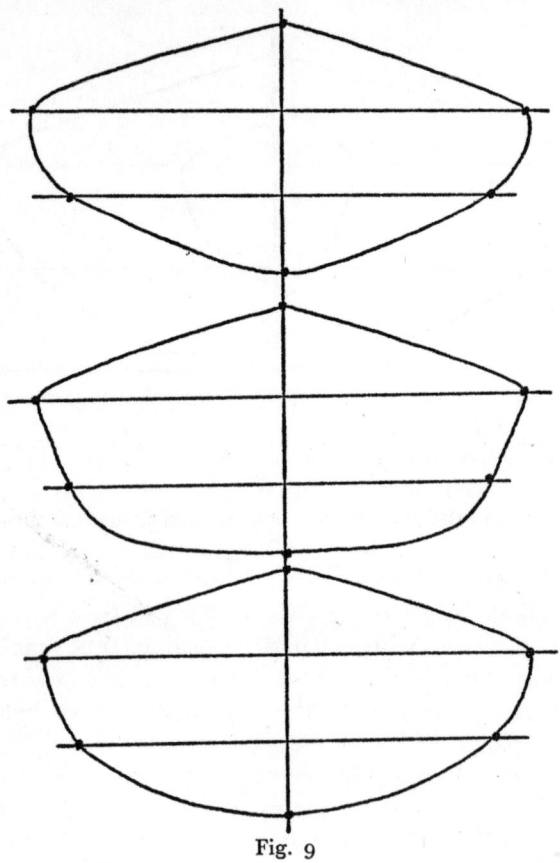

Fig. 9

carrier. The third section is that which is used in the rest of the drawings.

Drawing main lines (profile)

Measure the width of the paper available. Suppose it is 28 in., allowing a 1-in. margin both edges. Suppose the length of the boat is to be 14 ft. If we shorten the common interval to 2 in., instead of 1 ft., then we can get the whole length of the boat in at one-sixth scale for length. The drawing will be 28 in. (14 x 2 in.) long. Just fits. However, as we will be using full size offsets, this means that lines will be angling in fairly steeply towards the bow and stern, with six times the possibility of making errors.

There is an alternative choice, get a piece of paper 14 ft. long. I have never tried that, but I suppose with canoes it is feasible. However, if your memory is good, and you can recognise a line for what it is, or if you work in stages, you can reflect the boat upon itself at the half-way point, at the master section, and so extend the scale common interval from one-sixth down to one-fourth or even one-third of 12 in. Bear in mind that with fore and aft lines appearing on the same drawing, there may be superimposition, and closely parallel lines, which can be confusing. I prefer to use a one-fourth scale for common interval, accept the possibility of confusion, and thus get a fair degree of accuracy in a shorter sheet of paper, provided I can remember what's what.

Take the first sheet of paper, which has the one-tenth scale sketch of the canoe on it, and lay it out as follows. Up the right hand edge, about 1 in. in, draw a vertical line 12 in. high. Mark it off in 1-in. steps. Draw a line parallel to the bottom of the sheet and mark this off in 3-in. steps. Number the marks along the horizontal to correspond with the stations on the boat. As this boat is 14 ft. long, and assuming the master section is about the middle of the boat, number the fore stations 0 to 7, where 7 is the master section station. Then under these numbers put the aft station numbers, so that under 0 appears 14, under 1, 13; under 2, 12; and so on. 7 is the only common station.

Start with the gunwale line, on the profile. It may help you to use red pencil for profile, and black for plan, for example. Difficulty here is that red pencil is difficult to erase. I always use HB or 2B pencil lightly applied. Draw in the profile gunwale line at eight-inch height. (You could use 9 in., or 10 in., or 7.055 in., or whatever suits your purpose.) For the sake of illustration, I am using an eight-inch gunwale line and a 4-in. CWL. These two lines are now marked. A point in passing. Conventional hulls will have the waterline below the gunwale, which is usual in all displacement hulls. Planing hulls, like surf shoes, have probaby a 2-in gunwale height, with a 6 or 7-in. waterline. In that case the lines are reversed in order.

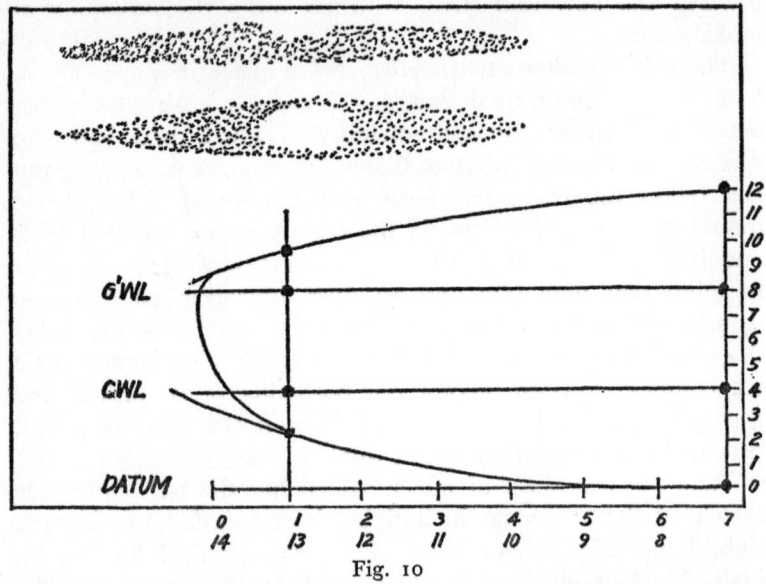

Fig. 10

The waterline is always a straight line in profile. In practice it never is, unless on dead calm water, but we make it so. The gunwale line on this illustration is straight, as is usual with most slalom-type, or river canoes. A good sea kayak will always have a fair degree of sheer, possibly 4 in. forward, and 2 in. aft. For simplicity we will have a straight gunwale, and now our thinking is beginning to produce a river touring canoe. It isn't long enough, nor does it have the necessary sheer for sea work.

Now consider the master section. The bottom of it touches the bottom of the vertical scale, so that point is at o vertically. The highest part of the section is, shall we say, 12 in. The height of the master section is marked off at 12 in. on the vertical scale. The gunwale and waterline points are already established at 8 in. and 4 in.

Now consider the bow section. At the first station we mark off the height. Say it is 10 in. The rocker is also marked off, probably 2½-in. It helps here to draw in a vertical at that station point. Gunwale and waterline points are already established.

Look at the sketch. Do you want a steady fall from the highest point to the bow, or do you want a deckline that is parallel to the waterline for, say, half its length, with a sort of droopy-snoot effect down to the bow? Or do you want a straight level deck line all the way along? That would give a high bow, possibly suitable in this case for moderate sea going work, as in an estuary where almost any boat is going to be a wet boat because of the short choppy seas one finds there. A high deck will help to throw off the water before it reaches the cockpit. But such a deck line isn't any good for slalom competition, as a high bow will tend to catch the gate poles and lose points for you. A high deck line is useful when cleaving through stoppers on rivers as in downriver racing. Well, all these points will be milling through your mind, and only experience will guide you with greater accuracy. Sometimes the illogicality of a decision made now does not reveal itself until the canoe has been used for some time in many conditions by many people. That's where 'mark two' becomes useful.

In this case I am going for a gentle down-curve towards the bow, a drop of two inches overall. In the same way I draw in the rocker curve. The relationship of bow rocker to stern rocker is quite important in the handling of a canoe. In a conventional stern-turning canoe, the bow rocker will start to rise from the lowest part of the hull to the bow rather further from the master section than the aft rocker will; but we are deciding on a river boat it seems, and it is not likely to be suitable for slalom, so it is better in that case to allow less rocker at the stern.

Now refer back to the stern section that was drawn earlier. It shows a lot more rocker than the bow section has. Its lowest point is higher up the vertical line than the bow section. Um, now what? Re-draw the stern section, leave it as it is, and put all this stern rocker in the last two or three feet? That doesn't make sense. If you have lots of rocker, it is for a purpose, and that is easy turning. Stop worrying, it is the bow rocker we are considering, but have half an eye on that stern rocker. It isn't making logical progress.

Draw in the bow rocker in pencil. Note that the bow shape has not yet been decided. I think we can leave that to the plug maker, with perhaps a glance at the one-tenth scale sketch to help him. Bow and stern end shapes owe more to carving skill and an eye for a line in harmony with the others on the boat. However, if this boat is to be used on rivers for touring, it will meet drifts of floating leaves, etc., from time to time. Autumn on the river Cherwell in Oxford comes to mind. A high bow with a gentle curve all the way up to it will allow leaves to drift away, but a deep square bow will catch and hold leaves. On the sea a deep bow with such a short boat would be more of an advantage. I think this boat is going to be meeting lots

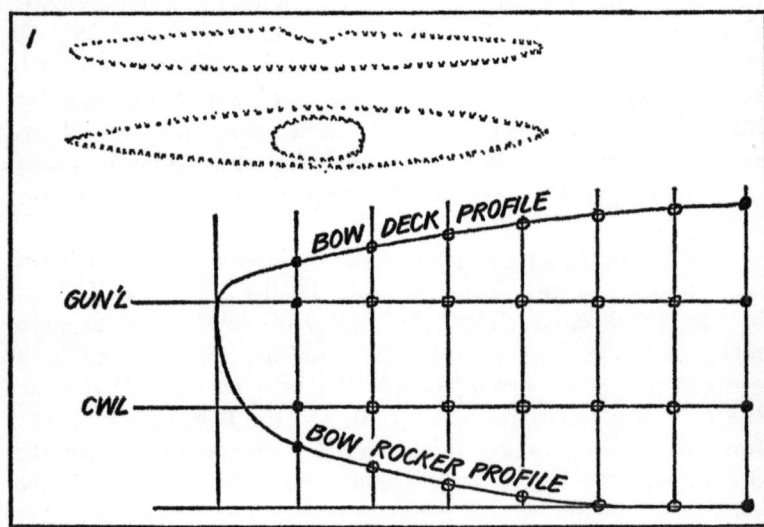

Fig. 11

of drifting leaves. Give it a gentle lifting bow. Note that on this drawing the curve seems steep, but in fact when the plug is made, the common interval is extended from three inches to twelve, so gradients are made less steep by a factor of four.

Now draw in verticals on all the stations. It would be better to draw these in ink, although every other line must be in pencil. There are now twenty-eight points to be transferred to the master section drawing on sheet two. These points all appear on the vertical line. I have ringed them to make them more obvious.

Having satisfied yourself that the two curved lines, the bow or fore deck and the fore rocker are both smooth and correct, and that the points where they cross the verticals corresponding to each station have been correctly transferred to the first drawing, you may then erase the pencil curves. However, you may prefer, as I do, to keep these lines in existence, so as not to lose them, in case you have to make an alteration to some other line later on which has a feed-back effect upon one of these lines. You would erase if you thought that the multiplicity of lines is going to confuse your eye. I sometimes wonder if by having all the lines co-existing on the sheet, I pick up some harmony from them, thus lending style to the boat. If so, it is quite unconscious.

Now draw the aft deck line and rocker line in the same way. Remember that we have still not sorted out the illogicality of the stern rocker. It may be that the thinking leading to this impasse is lacking logic. Lets try again.

1. It is to be a river canoe, being short, with a low bow, and a straight gunwale. The bow rocker is curved high to release leaves under it.
2. It has a fairly vee-bottom, lending speed and directional stability.
3. It has more 'dig' at the front than at the back, so it must be stern turning.
4. Where is it to be used? Who knows? Upper river stretches, with rapids and stoppers, or middle rivers with long calm stretches, or estuarial waters with short choppy waves? Will it be a big river with wide straight stretches,

or a small river with narrow gaps and fallen trees? Too many imponderables there.

Now there *must* be a decision on this stern rocker. Redraw the section, or allow the high degree of stern rocker allied to what is tending to be a straight running boat? Oh blow it! All boats are compromises. We'll have the section as shown. Now to draw the aft profile of the boat.

Use sheet one again. On this I have shown the stern profile inside the bow profile. The stations now run from 7, the master section station, to 14, the end of the line on which the canoe is being designed. In fact this canoe will not be 14 ft. long, it will be about 13 ft. 9 in., or possibly 13 ft. 10 in. If you do want to use this canoe in ranking slalom competitions, make sure that it is not shorter than approximately 13 ft. 3 in., or it will not satisfy competition regulations. It could be made 14 ft. long, but that would cause the bow and stern profiles to coincide on the drawings, and that might confuse the eye. To help, I have shown the lines we are not using as dotted. The lines we are concerned with are solid. Make sure you are using soft pencil lightly applied.

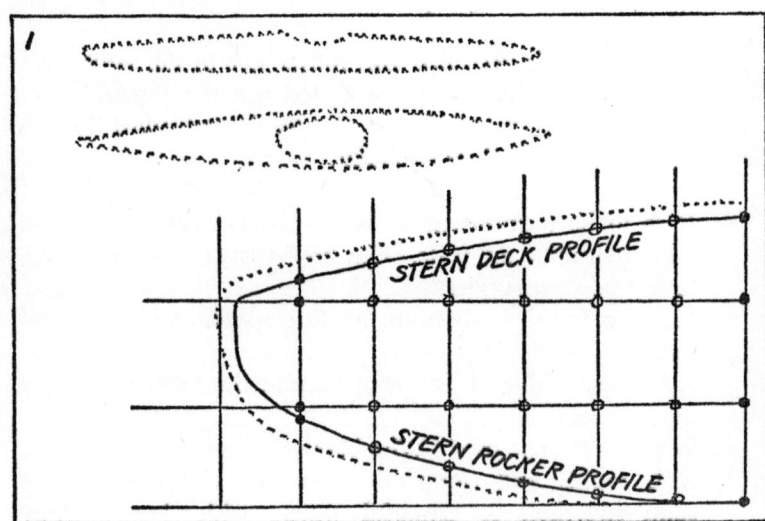

Fig. 12

Sketch in the stern deck profile, and the stern rocker profile. The solid black dots show the marks we already have, taken from the master section and stern section drawing on sheet two. The stern shape is shown almost straight up and down. Because of the more general use to which this primarily river boat may be put, it may be used with a rudder, and it is helpful to give the user a stern post which is straight up and down, or nearly so. Measurements can now be taken where the lines cross the station lines, and so we have another twenty-eight points to transfer to the section drawing on sheet two.

Incidentally, you will see that the stern deck profile starts lower down on station 7 than does the bow profile. This is because the cockpit coaming occupies this part of the canoe, and it is usual to give the cockpit rim an upward rake from the back to the front, hence the back is lower than the front. Another good practical reason is that if a cockpit has a low

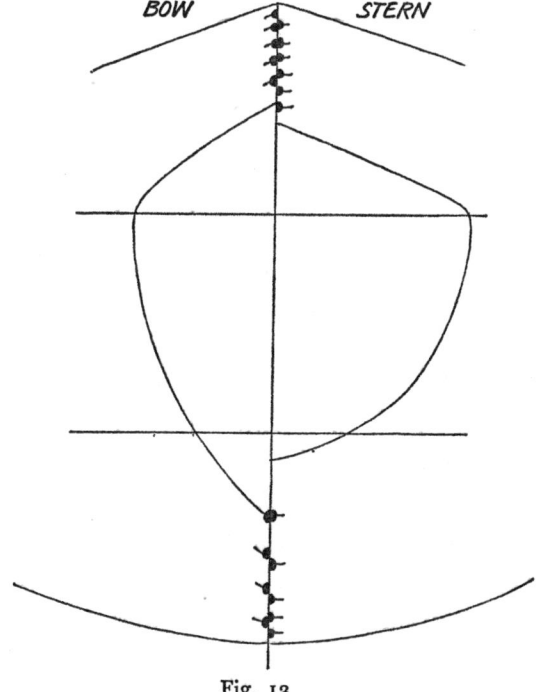

Fig. 13

back, then lay-back, or 'Steyr' rolls are easier.

At this stage, there is a concentration of points on the vertical centre line of the master section drawing. You can find yourself lost among a maze of dots. Therefore it is necessary to organise these points. The bow sections are to appear on the left of the line, the stern sections on the right. Mark these points by ticks from the centre line towards the side to which they refer. Figure 13 shows what I mean. You can also number these with a fine pencil to help you later.

Drawing main lines (plan)
It is now necessary to have available a grid the same as that used for the profile drawings. In fact I use the same grid on which the fore and aft profiles already appear. You can use a separate sheet, for simplicity, but you may lose some of the harmony which having all the lines together may lend to the drawings.

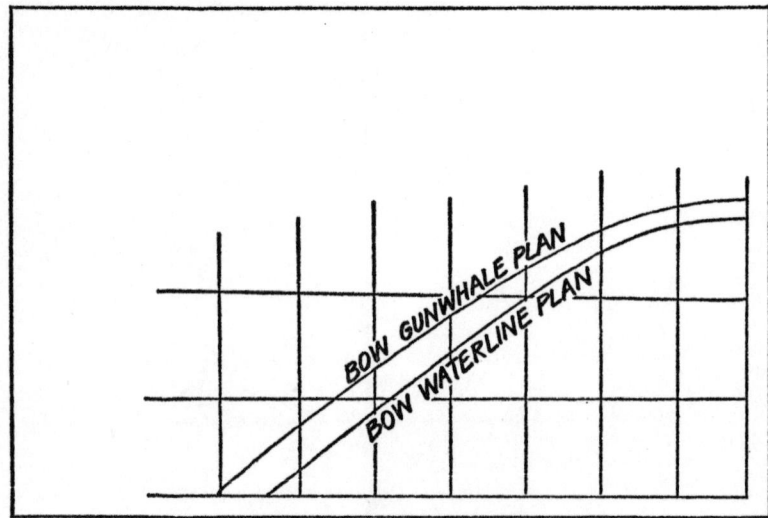

Fig. 14

The first line to be drawn is the fore or bow gunwale line. This must be parallel to the base line when it meets station 7, otherwise the plug maker will find a slight kink at this point which will have to be smoothed out which uses lots of filler and time. It is easier to smooth it out with eraser at the drawing stage. The majority of the curvature in the fore section usually takes place over the three stations 5, 6, and 7. The line is usually straight or slightly convex outward from the bow to section 5. To make a concave line here will give a sharp entry into the water, but there will probably be oddities of water flow where the concave section must turn into the convex curve on sections 5, 6, and 7. Also, to make a lean entry like this is to reduce the buoyancy of the fore sections, and so the bow will tend to dig in to head waves, or to 'Pearldive' in surf. Such a lack of buoyancy will require the cockpit to be moved further back, in order to obtain a better longitudinal balance. This in turn affects the widest part of the canoe which may now be at station 8 instead of 7, and so the whole basis of the drawing would now have to be changed. The grid on sheet 2 would need to run, for a 14-ft. canoe, 0/–; 1/–; 2/14; 3/13; 4/12; 5/11; 6/10; 7/9; and 8. I don't advise this change, in fact this thinking would have been done before the drawing commenced. But if you do have changes of mind at this stage, you must deal with the consequences. If such a change is essential, then far better to make changes now which might cost an hour or two, then have to make far more expensive changes later.

Having draw the gunwale line, now draw the fore waterline. Look at the master section and see how far out from the vertical centre line the waterline (4 in.) is. Mark off this measurement on the vertical line at the right side of the drawing grid on sheet 1. In a similar way mark off the waterline where it crosses station 1. With these two points, and keeping firmly in mind the idea that harmony is a good thing to go for, draw the waterline as parallel as one can to the gunwale line. Use soft pencil, lightly applied. The only inked-in lines at this stage, are the grid lines.

In passing, it is possible to play about with waterlines for various purposes. I would prefer to leave these ideas to you in later designs, after these basic steps have been mastered. One way is to bring the waterline outside the gunwale line. This is legitimate. It produces tumblehome, where the beam at the waterline is wider than the beam at the gunwale. If you get the opportunity to look at a racing K1, say an 'old fashioned'

Pointer, or Lancer, or Ranger, you will see that from above the plan view of the gunwale is diamond-shaped, with the widest part a fair bit aft of the cockpit. Turn the boat over and look very carefully at the waterline. Blot the gunwale line from your mind. It takes an effort of will to do it. You will see that the widest part of the waterline shape is at the middle point, or even forward of that. Look at the fore flanks of the hull. There is likely to be a very slight tumblehome here. Yet to look at the deck you would swear that the widest part of the canoe was aft of centre. Whereas in fact, that part which matters, the part in the water, is not so shaped. There are good reasons for this shape, it is not purely style.

The best basic rule I can pass on here is that simplicity is a good idea. Complicate and add weight, simplify and add lightness.

By now you have two lines which affect the fore part of the hull, in plan. The aft lines must also be drawn.

When you have dealt with this stage, there will be eight lines on the drawing: deck, rocker, gunwale, and waterline, distributed fore and aft. Figure 15 shows how it would look if

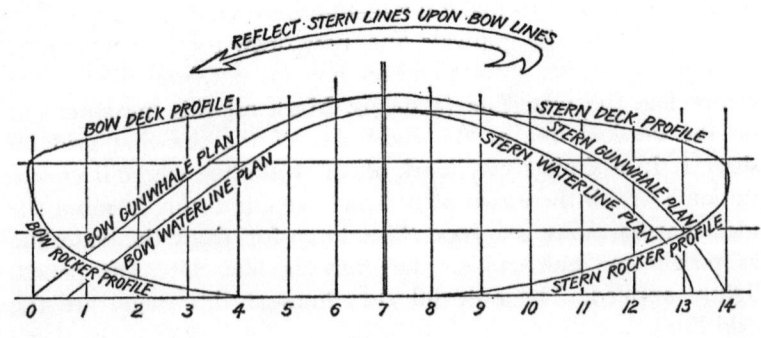

Fig. 15

these were drawn on one sheet of paper 60 in. long by 20 in. wide. In order to fit the more usually available sheets, which are 30 in. by 20 in., it is necessary to reflect the aft lines upon the fore lines, as in Fig. 16. You could have a sheet 60 in. long and 20 in. wide by fixing two sheets edge to edge, but be sure that the lines are in line, parallel and exactly spaced.

These lines are the basic minimum from which one can obtain the offsets necessary to draw all the sections.

It is now necessary to transfer all these points to the section drawing on sheet two. Take a section at a time. It is better to start with the sections nearest to the master section, so that the lines flow from the authority of that line. However, as section 8, or 6, is so close in the master section, it is easier for illustration to show the construction of section 2.

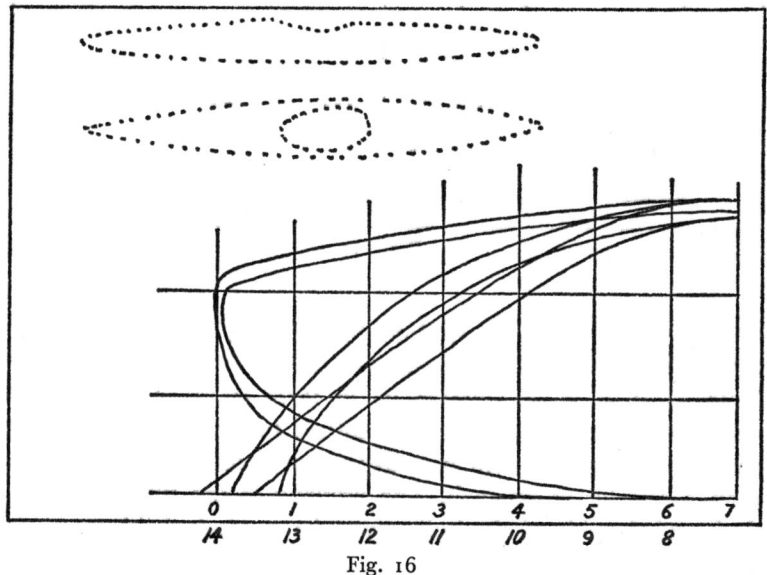

Fig. 16

Take sheet 1. Study station 2. Measure upwards from the base line to where the bow rocker line crosses. Transfer this measurement to sheet 2, measuring upwards on the vertical centre line from the base line. Now measure on sheet 1 the height of the deck line above the base line, and transfer that measurement to sheet 2.

Back to sheet 1, and measure from base to where the bow waterline crosses it. This measurement is transferred to sheet 2, but in this case the measurement is made from the vertical centre line horizontally towards the left along the line which represents the CWL (waterline). The point for the gunwale is

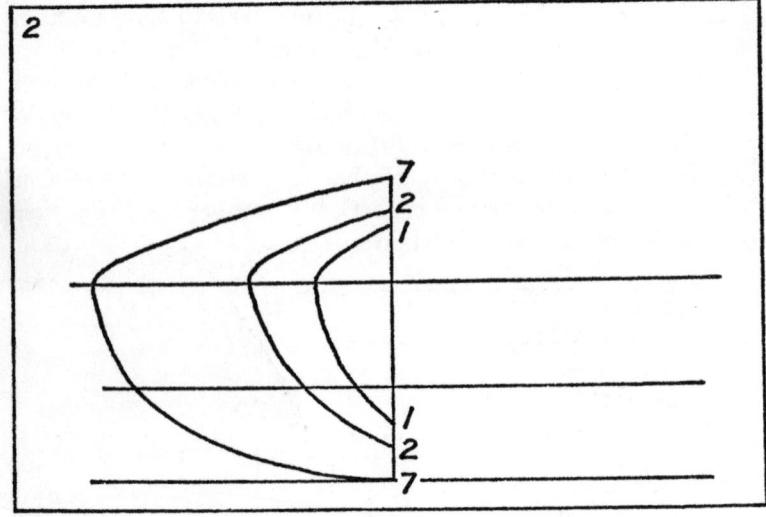

Fig. 17

measured in the same way. Note that all these measurements are full scale. There is no scaling up at this stage.

The section is now drawn in, in three stages. Draw in the deck, but remember that if you intend to work in grp in due course, the material will not take a curve of radius much less than a quarter of an inch. The drawing of the curve between deck and the side of the hull must take account of this requirement.

Now draw in the hull side down to the waterline. It is not possible to do this without reference to the curvature under the waterline, so it is often necessary to draw and re-draw these curves several times in order to get them to harmonise with each other. Work in soft pencil lightly applied, as before. Erase lightly, with a soft rubber.

In this way will each half section for the bow or fore part of the boat be drawn. It is at this stage that an eye for the harmony of the lines is essential. Whilst I took section 2 for example, the normal way to work is to start next to the master section and work outwards, so the fore sections would be measured off in the order 6, 5, 4, 3, 2 and 1. All these half sections are shown

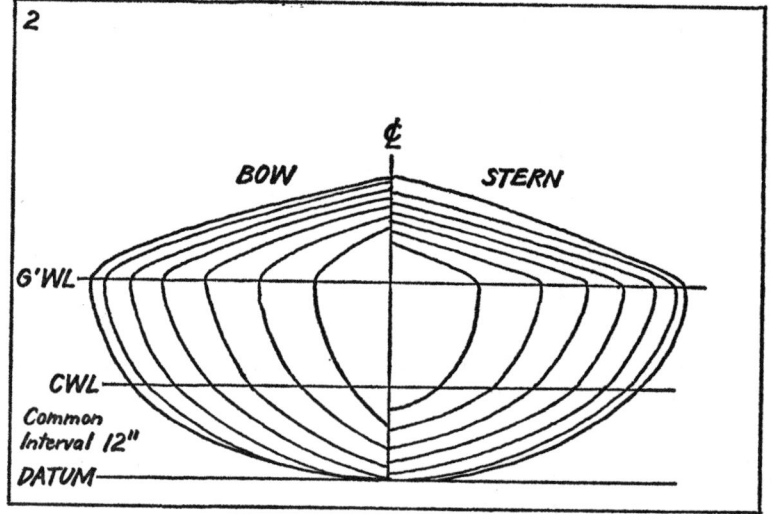

Fig. 18

on the left of the central vertical line on sheet 2. At this point, after the half sections have been drawn, one looks for signs of discordant lines (see page 55).

Finally, after much drawing, erasing, and redrawing, one has a set of lines, each section being full size, each separated by the common interval which is 1 ft. Look at it again and again, and seek out any irregularities. Once satisfied, then take a flexible curve, or a set of french curves, and ink in the various lines.

Effect of sheer on gunwale calculations

The book so far has dealt with a gunwale which curves in one plane only. It is supposed to have no sheer at all. However, if one introduces positive sheer (or negative, but I doubt if I would do that), the drawings must include this fact. It is shown as follows.

Suppose that it is a kayak-type of boat, with high raking bow, lots of bow sheer, and a steeply raked stem. The profile lines for the bow when put on the grid will look something like that shown on the drawing. When the rest of the drawing is done, and then the points are transferred to the full size section drawing, allowance must be made for this sheer.

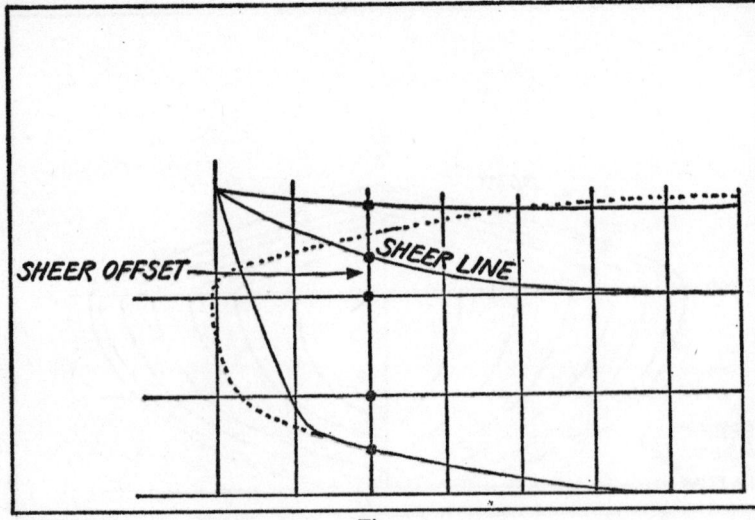

Fig. 19

First the horizontal offset is placed for a given section. This is marked on a horizontal line, as if there were no sheer at all, just as for the section drawing already discussed. However, reference is now made to the amount that the sheer line rises

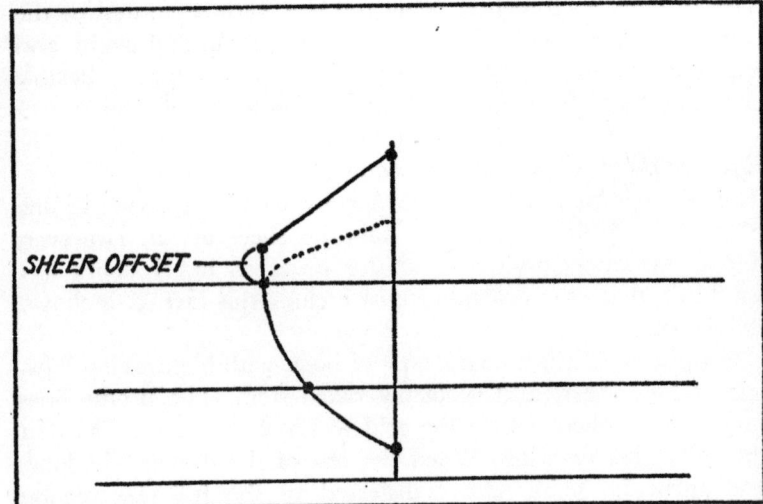

Fig. 20

above the horizontal line, and the dot is moved upwards from the horizontal to include this sheer. It is of course obvious that the whole shape of the boat is different. The deck line is moved up to be in harmony with this sheer. The horizontal offset is as for the example already given, both gunwale and waterline, and the rocker is the same. The dotted outline shows the profile of the case already described.

Incidentally it is simply coincidence that the section shape follows the same line from keel to waterline and from waterline to the old gunwale point. It is more likely that in the case of a different design of this type, that there would be less curvature from the sheer line to the waterline, and more curvature in the bottom, from waterline to keel. This effect is shown in Fig. 21, the outline so far offered being shown dotted, with the essential points as before. The new shape is radically different, and of course would start off with a completely different master section.

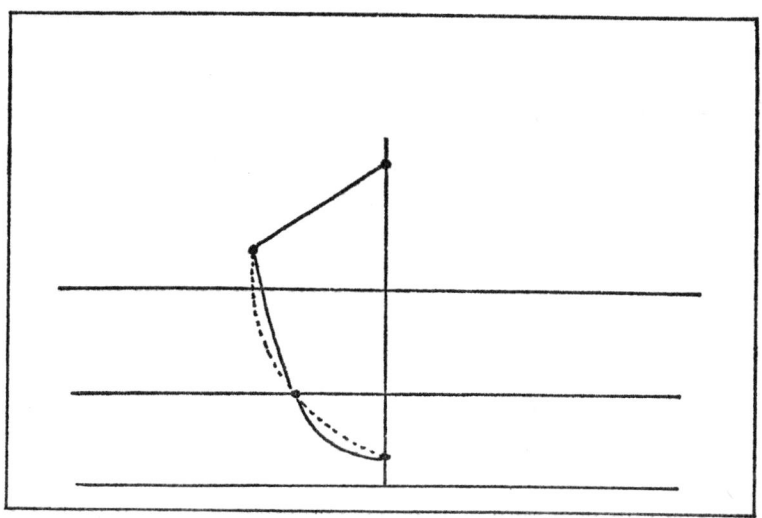

Fig. 21

Discussion of irregularities
In Fig. 22, you can see that one, the larger section, has a sharply turned gunwale edge. This may even be too sharp a turn for grp materials to take, and so this boat, however many

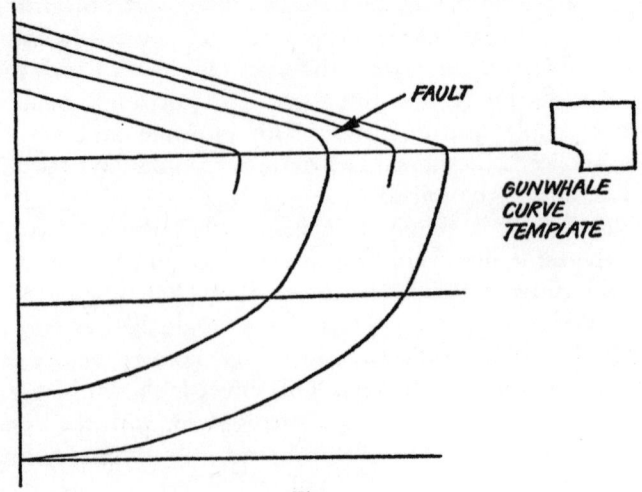

Fig. 22

were made, would be likely to produce time after time, bubbles under the gelcoat along the deck edge of the boat, just above the joint line. A sharp turn looks well if properly done, giving a trim high-light along the edge. With such a canoe laid well over on its gunwale as in a fast break-out on turbulent water, it would suddenly scoop water on to the deck, thus 'tripping up'. The effect on the paddler is most unsettling.

Now look at the smaller section. Note first that the turn from the deck to the hull side is a gentle curve, possibly three times the radius of the section already discussed. The material will take this curvature quite well, but think of the effect of a high-light along this edge. It will show a sharp clean, well-defined line near to the larger section, but it will become less sharp and more diffuse near to the smaller section. This will upset the eye, and look bad. It is bad! The amount of turn required is somewhere between the one and the other. A good way to get equal amounts of turn from deck edge to hull side on all sections, is to use a small piece of card and, for each section, cut out exactly the curvature required. Use this as a stencil on each section as you draw it.

Note another point about this section. Assuming the larger

section is the master section, note that the deck line on the smaller section converges on the line of the master section as it nears the gunwale edge. Putting in two other section lines each side helps to emphasise the fact that one is bound to get a hump in his deck about half way back from cockpit to end. It may seem trivial at this stage, but when you have built a plug with this fault in it, you realise that it is not trivial.

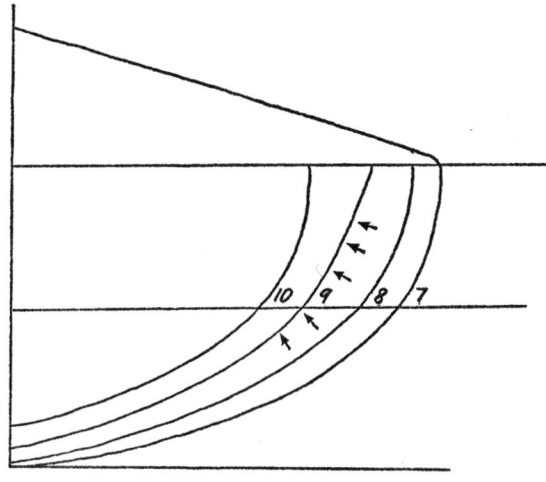

Fig. 23

Taking a part of the stern sections, numbers 7, 8, 9 and 10, either there has been an error of measurement here, or one of drawing. Section 7 being the master section will have been drawn first, so you cannot alter that now. Section 8 seems to harmonise well with it. The hull side follows the same slope and degree of curvature. Ignore section 9, and look at 10. It too follows the angle and curvature of 7 and 8. But 9 looks very odd at the waterline. If a smooth progressive curve is expected from 7 to 10, then the distances measured along the waterline between 7 and 8, 8 and 9, 9 and 10 would show a gentle geometrical progression, each gap being slightly more the further one goes from the master section. The gunwale points seem to be about right, as each gap between adjacent sections does indeed increase slightly the further one goes from the master section. The effect of this fault would be to produce an energy-consuming ripple in the waterflow along the side of the hull by section 9, because there would be a slight hollow in the curvature of the hull. When making the plug one would run one's hand over it, and feel the slight depression there. This would absorb lots of filler and time from the plug maker.

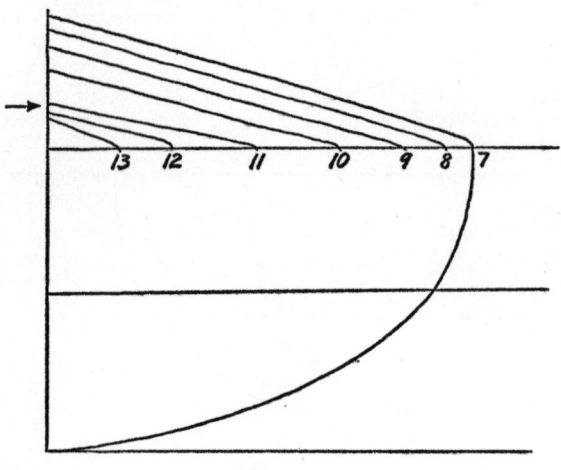

Fig. 24

Consider the deck ridge. This too should be a smooth curve, and this line is particularly noticeable when looking at the canoe. Look at the deck line on this sketch. The sections show a slight progression from 7 to 10, quite properly, which indicates a gentle down-curve on the rear deck. There then follows a sharp drop to section 11, and sections 12 and 13 have been crammed close together in order not to upset the gunwale curvature. The result here would be a sharp drop in the deck line, followed by a sway-backed effect between this sag in the deck and the stern. In practice this would look most unsightly. However, it is permissible to have considerable changes in section shapes, particularly near to the ends when done deliberately, as with an eskimo kayak. Figure 25 shows how the deck line of a boat like 'Anas Acuta' looks at the stern.

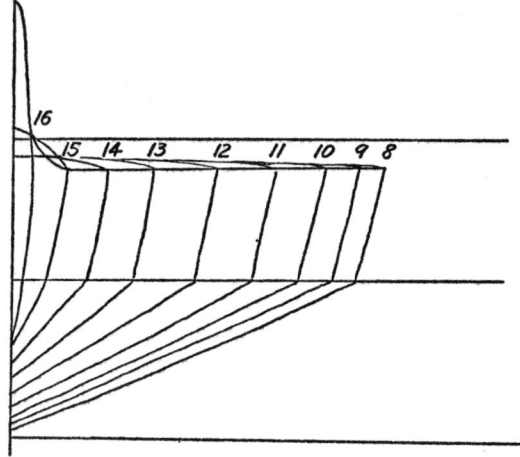

Fig. 25

Several points to note about Fig. 25. One is that, as a result of a drawing error, I have given it far too much dead rise. The angle upwards of the hull bottom from keel line to chine line is far too steep. Such a boat would be hell to balance in all but a calm sea, and even that would be fraught with possibilities. I hasten to point out that Anas Acuta does not have these unpleasant characteristics.

Next point is that the gunwale line from the master section towards the rear shows a curving in of the gunwale line from 8 to 10, it then runs dead straight from 10 to 13, and starts to curve outwards again from 13 to the end. This will give a hollow line to the gunwale about 3 or 4 feet ahead of the stern.

The deck is almost flat, having a gentle camber of about an inch, but just in front of the stern post it starts to rise up into the characteristic tail of Anas Acuta. Note the rocker line of this boat. It rises progressively from master section to the stern, but just in front of, and under the stern, it almost flattens out. This was necessary to give AA its directional stability. Without that extra dig at the stern it weather-cocked in a side wind. With about an inch added at the very stern, taken about 2 to 3 ft. forward as a slightly emphasised keel line, it stopped that drift on the first model, and that was corrected before the kayak was produced commercially.

Note the high raised tail at the stern. Various reasons could be given for this characteristic of this type of boat. Not all hunting kayaks had it. Kayak-building in a village was usually the job of a retired seal hunter. He may have built it in as his trade mark. However, in winter time when the sea ice closed the fiords, the hunter would strap a small sledge under the cockpit of the kayak, using the cockpit as a hold-all, and walk across the ice to the sea edge where hunting was still possible. The high standing tail made an excellent handle by which to grasp, pull, and direct this kayak on a sledge. If you want to see the original which gave rise to the development of this very popular boat, see *The Bark Canoes and the Skin Boats of North America*, Fig. 21.

Finally, it may be helpful to you to note that this system of obtaining a set of sections is not the usual method of obtaining a set of lines as in yacht design. To obtain a further cross check on lines so far obtained, it is possible to take vertical longitudinal slices out of the boat, and the outline of these slices where they meet the hull skin gives a series of lines called buttock lines. These are profiles taken at certain intervals from the centre

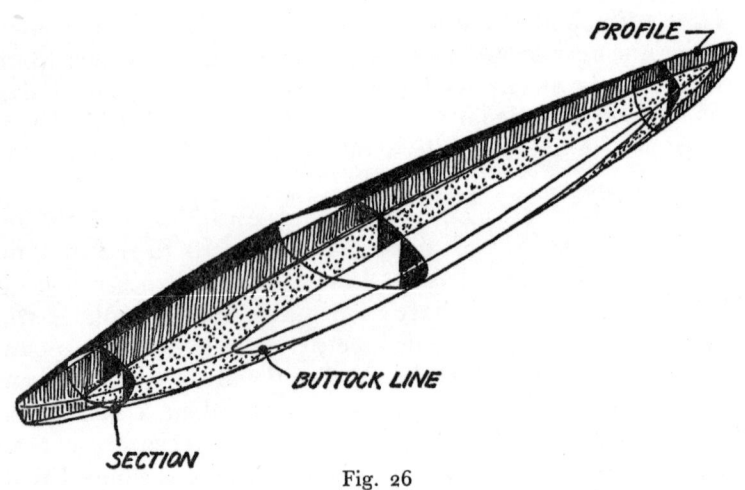

Fig. 26

line of the boat, in the case of canoes it might be at 3-in. intervals, or 4-in. intervals.

F. S. Kinney in the book *Skene's Elements of Yacht Design,* 1962 edition, p. 14, describes the sequence in which he obtains the lines for a yacht. It is his own method, or at least, a method which suits his way of working. The requirements of yacht design are much more complicated than those of canoe design, but experience does inform the mind in much the same way.

Therefore, although Frank Goodman (one of the book's critics, and who designs canoes) recommends the use of buttock lines, I have not used them, and find that I obtain useful drawings from which I can turn out useful canoes. I suppose that what I am offering in this book is a way of designing a canoe which is about as simple as one can do it; to be more sophisticated requires more information, and that one can obtain from the many books on the subject of yacht design.

CHAPTER FIVE

Calculation, Presentation, Adaptation

It is not essential to work out these figures or to draw a curve showing the relationship of waterline and displacement. If you don't like playing about with figures, then you don't have to do so. But do take warning, that at this stage you can start to 'prove' your design, and to make some simple approximations to the final likely performance of the canoe, before you commit resources of time and money to making a plug, which is the costly part of grp canoe building. I always feel more certain about the canoe when I make these calculations which are simple enough, and the finished appearance of your drawing is enhanced by a simple curve showing, to those who can read it, a lot about the boat.

As you read this section on calculations, you may recognise the possibility of using an instrument like a planimeter, which traces over curves and tells you the area under it; or by using the various rules used in displacement calculations, the trapezoidal, or Simpson's, or Tchebycheff's rules; or by using calculus, or nowadays feeding a computer with facts and letting it design your boat. What I have done is to address myself to the average person who knows canoes and isn't very knowledgeable about calculation methods.

The method I have used gives an error of 2–5 per cent under the proper value of the displacement calculation. So if, as in this case, I get an answer of 204 lb. at a 4-in. waterline, then really it will be nearer 210 lb. The variation is so small, affecting the waterline by about 1/20 of an inch, that it can be ignored.

Using Figure 27 as an illustration, the half section is the master section, the waterline is the 4-in. line, and the squares are 1-in. squares. We want the area bounded by the curve of the half section, the 4-in. waterline and the vertical centre line, The top line gives

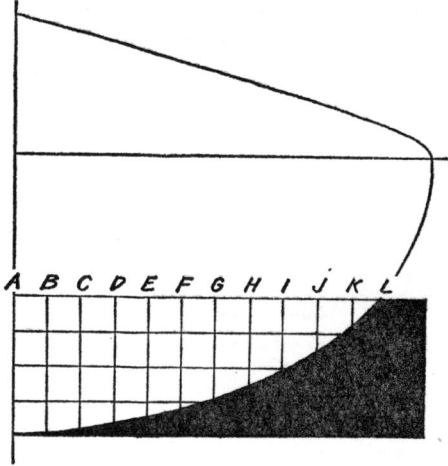

Fig. 27

9 full squares plus		9/10		1/3
The second line gives 8 full squares plus 3/4			1/4	
The third line gives (almost) 6 full				
squares plus		3/4		1/4
The fourth lines gives 1 full square plus				
(ignoring the little bit)		3/4	9/10	1/4

This all adds up to 24 full squares plus 1/3 plus 1/2 plus 3 (1/4+3/4) plus 2 (9/10), which I make to be 24+5/6+ 3+1+4/5, or 29 and 2/3 (approx.).

Having found the area of this half section, it is now listed, as 29 and 2/3 square inches. This is the simplest method known as 'counting squares'.

The trapezoidal method is as follows. A trapezium is a four-sided figure, two sides of which are parallel. Its area is half the sum of the lengths of each of the parallel sides multiplied by the perpendicular distance between them. In this special case for canoe design, one of the sides which is not parallel to its opposite side is drawn at right angles to the two parallel sides. Taking the illustration, look at the areas bounded by each of the 1 in. verticals. Each is nearly enough, a trapezium. The two verticals are the two parallel sides, and part of the water-line is the perpendicular between them. There is a common interval between each of the pairs of verticals, which in this case is 1 in. Each of the verticals has been labelled from 'A' to 'L'.

The area of the trapezium between the vericals 'A' and 'B' is ½ of (A+B) multiplied by 1 in. The area of the next in order is ½ of (B+C) multiplied by 1 in. and the next is ½ of (C+D) multiplied by 1 in., and so on.

Taking out common factors we have

$$1 \text{ inch} \times \tfrac{1}{2} (A+B+B+C+C+\ldots\ldots+K+K+L)$$

or,

$$\begin{matrix}1 \text{ inch}\\ \text{(Common)}\\ \text{interval}\end{matrix} \times \left[\frac{(A+L)}{2}+(B+C+D+E+F+G+H+I+J+K) \right]$$

This can be more generally expressed as the area of the whole is the common interval multiplied by (half the sum of the end ordinates (the verticals) plus the sum of all the other ordinates).

Using Fig. 27 again, and taking rough measurements from it, the lengths of the ordinates appear to be, expressed in tenths,

A+L=	4+0
B	3 9/10
C	3 8/10
D	3 6/10
E	3 4/10
F	3 2/10
G	2 9/10
H	2 5/10
I	2
J	1 5/10
K	8/10

Applying the rule, this gives

$$\frac{4+0}{2} + 22 + \frac{9+8+6+4+2+9+5+5+8}{10}$$

$$2+22+56/10 \text{ which equals } 29.6 \text{ in.}$$

Or,

This compares well with the result we had by counting squares, which gave an area of 29 and 2/3 in., and indicates an error of approx. 2 per cent under.

From either of these measurements we find that the area of the half section is about $29\frac{1}{2}$ square inches. This is listed. Also the list includes all the areas for the half sections in a complete canoe hull at a 4-in. waterline. (These are roughly calculated for the purpose of this example. They have no relation to a real canoe). Note that the areas are listed from master section to bow and master section to stern, separately. This is in order to find the longitudinal centre of gravity later.

Station	7	6	5	4	3	2	1	Total
Area	29.5	27.2	24.5	20.8	15.8	9.2	1.5	128.5
Station	7	8	9	10	11	12	13	
Area	29.5	28.5	26.5	23.2	18.4	12.5	3.8	142.4

Now, using the trapezoidal rule applied in a similar way to bring areas up to volumes, we have the following calculation, which applies to the front of the canoe. Total half volume = Common interval x half sum of end areas plus sum of all other areas.

This is, $12 \times [\frac{1}{2}(1.5+3.8)+(9.2+15.8+\ldots+18.4+12.5)]$

Or

$$12 \times (\frac{5.3}{2}+236.1)$$

(This is the volume in cubic inches of half the canoe. To bring it up to the correct amount, double it.) It becomes:

$$\text{Volume} = 12 \times (5.3+472.2)$$
$$= 12 \times 477.5 \text{ (cubic inches)}.$$

This should be expressed in cubic feet for ease of handling. It now is:

$$\text{Volume} = \frac{12 \times 477.5}{12 \times 12 \times 12} \text{ cubic feet}.$$

However, it is the displacement of the canoe at this waterline that I need to know. In fresh water, one cubic foot of water weighs about 62.5 lb. So, the sum now becomes:

c

$$\text{Displacement} = \frac{12 \times 477.5 \times 62.5}{12 \times 12 \times 12} \text{ lbs weight}$$

Which is a great big unwieldy sum, and nowhere near dead accurate. Clearly a 12 will cancel with a 12 above and below the line. That leaves us with 477.5 multiplied by a fraction, $\frac{62.5}{144}$. If this fraction is worked out to three figures, it is expressed as a decimal as 0.434. If it is made into a fraction, 3/7, its value as a decimal is 0.429. This is an error of 1 per cent less approx. Which is acceptable, for the ease of working with a sum which can be generally expressed as :

The displacement of the canoe hull is the sum of the areas of its sections according to the trapezoidal rule, multiplied by 3/7, where the common interval is 12 in. and the areas are expressed in square inches, and the answer is expressed in pounds weight.

Having arrived at what might be called Byde's inaccurate constant, definitely in the shipwright's order of calculation, the figures I have been working with produce a result, 204.6 lb. weight. That is the displacement of the hull of this canoe at a waterline of 4 in.

Imagine now the finished canoe. It weighs about 35 lb., complete. The paddler weighs about 11 st., shall we say, which is 154 lb. His equipment may weigh another 10 lb., that is paddle, lifejacket, clothing, etc. So, we have a situation where, at a designed waterline of 4 in. on this canoe, it will carry 154+10+35, plus a load of 5.6 lb. So, it looks as if we have designed fairly accurately, a river-type canoe which will be just about on its normal waterline with an 11 st. paddler and no extra load, such as camping gear. This is fine. The design is about right, not far out, and so consideration can be given to building the plug knowing that it will be about right. First, however, we must obtain two more waterline calculations. I usually add a half inch and an inch to the first waterline, so the two new calculations are made for a $4\frac{1}{2}$-in. waterline and a 5-in. waterline. It is not necessary to again calculate everything from the beginning, as a simple addition on each of the sections shapes, by counting squares, usually suffices. The results in this case may be as follows. Waterline $4\frac{1}{2}$ in., displacement 246 lb. Waterline 5-in., displacement 292 lb.

Given these results, it is possible to construct a buoyancy curve, with the horizontal scale showing the draught, and the vertical scale the displacement. This typically produces a curve, through origin, as shown in Fig. 28. I try always to give my curves the

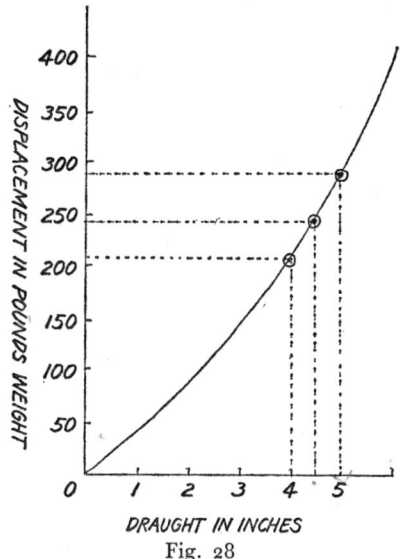

Fig. 28

same scale, so that the horizontal scale is at 1 in. per inch of waterline, and the vertical scale is 1 in. per 50 lb. of displacement. This allows me to superimpose these scales when drawn on tracing paper, so that I can compare older designs with the new one.

Finally, in the calculations, it is necessary to work out where the centre of gravity is to be at the chosen waterline. In this case, it looks as if the 4-in. waterline will do very well; but if for example, it turned out that on a 4-in. waterline there was a displacement of only 180 lb., then clearly the actual waterline in use might be nearer $4\frac{1}{2}$ in. In that case the calculation would have to be done at that waterline.

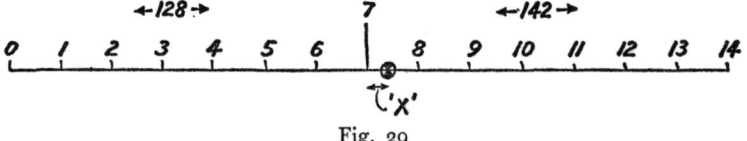

Fig. 29

Assuming that the figure we have is satisfactory, you will see that the sum of the areas of the half sections for the fore part is 128.5, and that for the rear part is 142.4. We can ignore the decimal fractions here. Using the theory of moments, and assuming that the ratio of the areas we have will be in the same proportion as the ratio of displacement fore and aft, then the balance point longitudinally will be aft of the master section. Let the distance from station 7 (the station where the master section is) be X feet. Then we have an equation, an approximation only, which is

$$128 \text{ x } (7+X) = 142 \text{ x } (7-X)$$

Worked out, X is very nearly 11/30 ft. Therefore, this design produces a longitudinal centre of buoyancy which is 4.4 in. behind station 7. Assuming that the centre of gravity of the average paddler is about half way between knee cap and hip joint, when sat in the usual, slightly bent-forward position, and

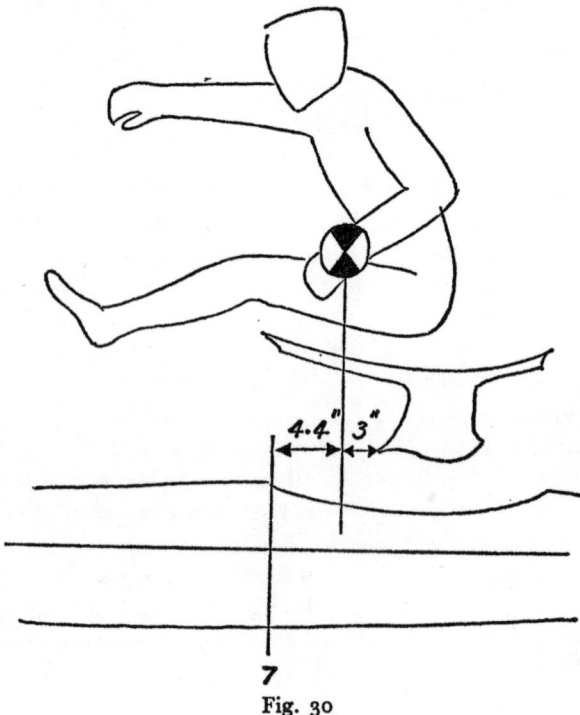

Fig. 30

assuming that the front of the average canoe seat is just under the crutch, then the centre of gravity will be about 2 to 3 in. in front of the front of the seat. In this case you would arrange the cockpit rim on the deck so that the front edge of the seat is between $6\frac{1}{2}$ and $7\frac{1}{2}$ in. behind station 7.

Now for a small confession. I regularly apply these approximations and can see no good reason to question their usefulness Yet, quite often when designing a canoe, I find that I have managed to balance the things so that it is tail light and bow heavy. In other words it will dig its bow into the water and the tail end will swing about. The acid test of this on a sea kayak is to try it in a side wind. If it is properly balanced it will be neutrally balanced across the wind. If it is tail light it will point bows to wind, i.e. weathercock. The opposite case I have never known, where the bows are light. Now, I should point out that an easy moving stern is a good thing for river work where manoeuvrability is required. But a sea kayak must be balanced across the wind. The intention with this boat is to use it mostly for river work, possibly for fairly fast straight line work when touring. I think I will leave this calculation where it stands. But if it were a sea kayak and I had come this far, knowing my ability to get it tail light, I would put the estimated centre of longitudinal balance about 3 in. further back yet, perhaps as much as 6 in. if the kayak were 18 ft long.

There is no science to back these figures. I know a man on Arran who makes 20-ft. fishing boats, curragh, whose measuring sticks are his forearm, his hammer shaft, the widths of one, two, and three fingers. The boats work.

Arrangement of cockpit

Whilst we are considering the cockpit and its position, it will be useful to consider the paddler. Figure 31 is a footrest's 'eye' view of the paddler when upside down and all wound up to roll. I must confess to pure imagination here. The nervous paddler will have his heels tightly jammed together, and his knees will be crammed up tight to the foredeck. His toes will find a certain prehensile quality and curl around the footrest bar. He will be developing some tension in his muscles in his legs.

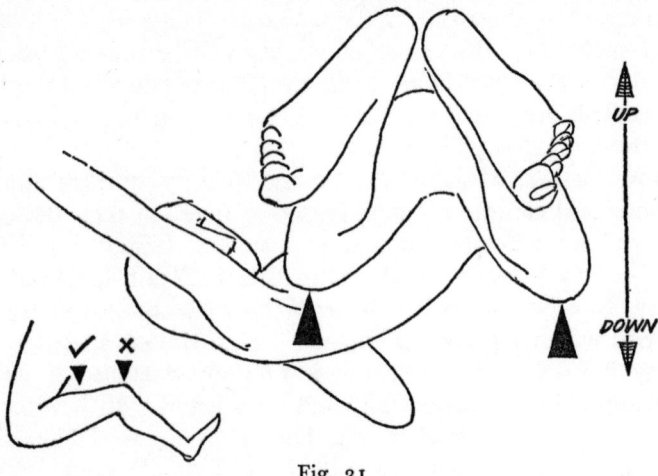

Fig. 31

Now feel your knee. It's bony, and only thinly covered with skin. Feel your mid thigh. On top. It is muscly, and covered with plenty of meat, you cannot feel your thigh bone. Suppose you are hanging upside down in a canoe cockpit, with your chest and head under water. They will be supported by the buoyancy of the water, and will have relatively little weight. However, your legs and lower body are jammed into the cockpit in air, (supposing you are using a spray deck) and so slightly more than half your weight is resting on the underneath of the deck. There is no weight on the seat or floor. Add to this the fact that you are driving your knees up tight to the deck and there will be about three-quarters of your body weight pressing on the underneath of the foredeck on two small points, your knee caps. Suppose each knee cap has an area when under pressure, of half a square inch. Suppose your body weight is 168 lb. then I calculate that each knee cap is experiencing a pressure of 126 psi. It makes your eyes water. That is about four times the pressure in a car tyre.

A better idea is to so arrange the cockpit that your thighs take the weight of your body, and you do this by bringing the cockpit rim down towards the thighs; by putting in wooden bars, commonly called 'roll bars' to deepen the rim of the cockpit; or by raising the foredeck over the knees so that they cannot touch the foredeck. This is done usually by putting on knee blisters, so called. They are not bulges into which you fit your knees, merely a local raising of the deck.

Drawing presentation

If a job is worth doing, it's worth doing well. So saith the old and wise craftsman. I've met a lot of them and they all say the same thing eventually. Even I am beginning to say it. I don't claim wisdom or age, but the truth of it is self-evident. You should have a sheet of squared paper with a number 1 on it, and the one-tenth plan and profile sketches, and the plan and profile full scale offsets. It will probably have collected pencilled notes, and lists of figures. The second sheet, number 2, will have the full size sections drawn on it, with the displacement, or buoyancy curve. The backs of the sheets will probably have the lists of numbers associated with the calculations for the displacement curve. The general impression I find is one of ordered confusion. It is not realistic to try to work from such a mess as this. The act of tracing through the section shapes one after the other when building the plug will cut the section drawings to ribbons, and the drawing is then lost, to be re-created only at a considerable expense of time and effort. The obvious thing to do is to print the drawings, in fact have at least four copies made. The best way to do this, I find, is to trace the lines required on to tracing paper (not linen) and take the tracing to a printer and have it copied. If I were in a strange town, or had no contacts that I could call on to copy these drawings, I would go to the nearest shop that sold drawing instruments and paper, and ask there; and if they didn't know where to get drawings copied I would look in the yellow pages of the telephone directory under 'Draughtsmen and Tracers'.

First, though, one must produce a useful tracing. On this must appear the one-tenth plan and profile; the full size section shapes; a note as to the common interval between sections; the buoyancy or displacement curve, and a note as to who designed and drew it, and when it was done. Finally a name is a useful thing to have, so brood on it.

The way in which to obtain the tracing is simple enough. First you need a piece of tracing paper, good quality, about

2 in. bigger all around than the final drawing required. If you work on a sheet 20 in. by 30 in., then the tracing paper should be 24 in. by 34 in. Draw an ink border within which the drawing will appear. This is so that lining up will be made easier as the drawing progresses. Lay the tracing paper over the one-tenth plan and profile sketches, and pin, or clip, or as I do, staple the waste edge of the tracing paper to the paper underneath. About 5 or 6 fixing points will do. Now, using the french curves or the flexible curve, ink the outline on to the tracing paper. Try and keep these well to the left of the sheet, not more than an inch down from the top border, and not more than an inch in from the left border. This allows room for the other details which must go on the sheet. You can also close up the plan to the profile if you like, with minimum distance between these, say 1 in., or even ½ in. The lines shown should be datum, waterline, deck and keel line, and gunwale. Now unfasten the sheet and do the section drawing.

Place the tracing paper over the sheet on which the section shapes appear. Organise it so that the centre line on the sections is dead on the centre vertical line on the tracing paper. You draw this in lightly in pencil on the tracing paper. Clip the two sheets together as before and start to trace through the section shapes in ink. I use a Rotring 0.6 mm drawing pen. This is a longish business but must be done with care and accuracy, because this series of section shapes will give the canoe its eventual shape after the plug maker has done his work, guided by your drawing. In my case that's me and me, and I can always curse myself for sloppy work if I wish. It is remarkable just how carefully the plug maker looks at a drawing after the first two or three boats, for he now knows what to look for, and what faults he may find. There is no way in which to shorten this business, except to do it, and find out.

Having now drawn the section shapes, copy the buoyancy curve on to the tracing, in the space in the top right corner. There should be just enough room there. Bottom right draw a box 4 in. by 2 in. Now use a lettering kit, either stencils or 'Letraset' and put on to the drawing the following words, for they are all that are required. More would be superfluous.

Name
Bow
Stern
Common Interval 12 in.
CWL
Displacement in pounds weight
Draft in inches
Designed by . . .
Drawn by . . .
Date . . .

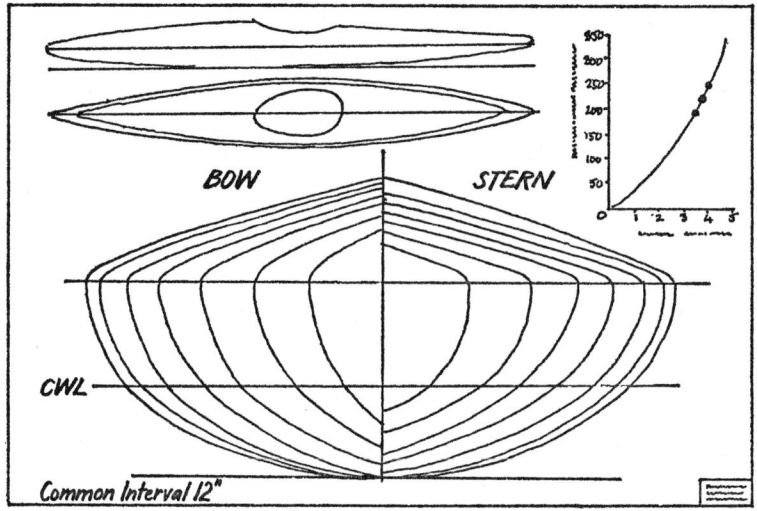

Fig. 32

You may find that you have ink smudges on the tracing. Wait until they are dry, and then scrape them off with the edge of a razor blade held vertically and used lightly. No need to do the whole thing all over again, for in the printing process the small smudges are overlooked by the machine and only strong black lines come through. So do take care that the lines you use are strong and black. Even the pen I use is near to being too thin. Red ink is useless, it simply doesn't register on most copying machines. To store the drawing, obtain a cardboard tube and roll it up. If you don't have one, you can if you use rolls of glass fibre take the tube out of the centre of such a roll. As a last resort, roll the tracing up in a whole newspaper, but never never fold it.

You now have the designer's intentions on paper, enough for a plug maker to make his plug for grp work, but the information given is not enough if the canoe is to be made in plywood or lath and canvas. The builder will have to make another set of drawings from these.

Some of the considerations which may affect your decision on drawings are as follows.

GRP work. If you are doing the work yourself, and if you have access to another set of moulds already made, you can take a small section of deck from that and graft it into your new plug, and so have a suitable fixing hole for your cockpit, which is simply copied from the old one. However, if you have done the drawing for a commercial plug maker, and he has never used a canoe before, still less made one, he will require lots of detail sketches for the cockpit and deck arrangements, and you may have to spend some time with him on repeated visits to keep him right. I did this with one canoe, and the plug maker put the knee bulges in the right place, but made them so high that you could almost use them as turrets for guns. It looked a bit of a freak that one did, and the deck line was too flat, so that a heavy wash of water up the foredeck would flatten it inwards, so causing flexion cracking along the gunwale edge. This was of course cured, but the degree of slope of a deck is instinct in a canoe user, he knows just how much a canoe will take before caving in.

Canvas canoes. I thought that my time with lath and canvas canoes was long past, but it has just been suggested to me by a member of the College who spent some time in a remote Indian school, that they would be very pleased to have a set of drawings for lath and canvas canoes for use on their local river, which floods now and then, so as to allow the schoolchildren and staff to help with immediate rescue and communication work. Glass and resin is out of the question, (a) because there isn't any, and (b) because it is so hot that storage at less than 20°C. without refrigeration is just not possible. However, they can obtain materials for canvas canoes quite easily. In that case the designer's drawings I have described to you can be used to obtain the frame shapes that canvas canoes require.

Plywood canoes. Much the same problem is found, a further set of drawings being required.

The following method is suitable to convert a set of designer's drawings into construction drawings for lath and canvas.

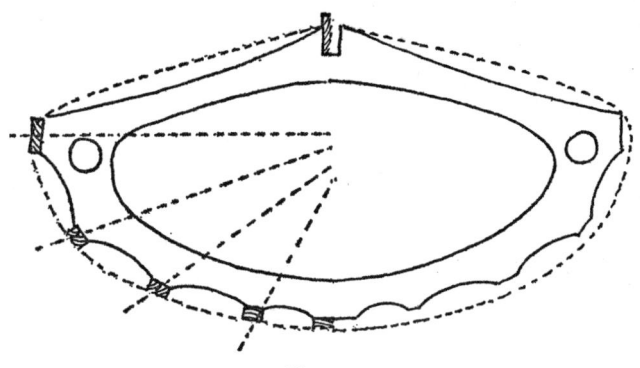

Fig. 33

Take the designer's drawings, and decide how many stringers are required. There must of course be a pair of gunwales, and a keel, although sometimes it is better to do without a single keel and install a twin keel one piece to each side of the centre. Familiarity with canvas canoe construction will guide your thinking on that. The more stringers there are the more closely will the canvas conform to the designed shape. Incidentally, because of the bagging inwards under pressure between stringers, the canoe will tend to sit lower in the water and will also have much more directional stiffness than a smooth bottomed grp canoe would have. Percy Blandford's books on canvas construction are the best source of information on this method of construction. (*See* Bibliography.)

Draw lines which radiate from the bow (or stern) posts more or less equally spaced across the hull part of the drawing. Now, using carbon paper, trace the outline shape of the section being drawn, on to another sheet of paper, ensuring that the stringer points are also marked. Draw in the shape required for the frame. This assumes that it is to be cut from marine plywood. Note how the frame curves away between stringers, so as to allow the canvas to bag inward. Note that at the wider frames, the paddler must sit, so that plenty of room must be allowed for him to get his legs in, without at the same time so reducing the width of the frames that they are weakened.

In this way all the frame shapes required can be drawn. It is not necessary to put a frame at every foot interval; 2 ft. intervals should be enough, with five or possibly six frames to a 14-ft. canoe.

CHAPTER SIX

Building a Plug

There are many ways to make a plug. I have made a plug from section shapes screwed to a base plate with the spaces between filled with coke and then modelling clay. It worked, but it was very difficult. Also, I have used strips of wood carefully fitted to strong frames, so as solidly to plank the plug with stringers. This method is so long and tedious to all but the professional plug builder, that by the time the job is finished, it has warped and cracked and lost its accurate shape. The method I use now is cheap, accurate, and quick.

Take a copy of the designer's drawing that you have made. Do not take the only copy, because the process will ruin the drawings you will use in construction. Obtain some carbon paper, four A4 size sheets. You will also need a sheet of $\frac{3}{4}$-in. blockboard, about 6 ft. by 3 ft. should do. A spine is required. I have used 3-in. square timber, but by far the best is a piece of scaffold tube, dead straight, and clean, about 2 ft. longer than the finished canoe is to be. The building place requires two trestles to support the tube, and some points of support overhead, in line with the tube, as the spine starts to bend with the weight of the sections being placed on it. Four full length stringers are needed, an industrial stapling machine, and lots of sheets of strong cardboard which you can get from the supermarket. It is assumed that you have grp materials also.

Find the exact diameter of the tubular spine, and draw a circle on the drawing of the sections. This circle has the same diameter as the spine. It is necessary to organise it so that the circle is within each of the section shapes, and leaves enough material on each section to allow the tube to be threaded through without breaking the section. This affects the ends only. You can ignore the last foot of each end at this stage.

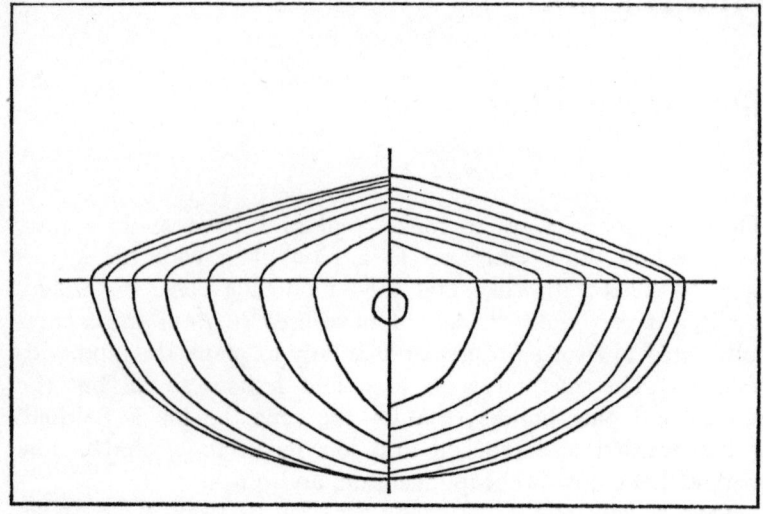

Fig. 34

One by one the section shapes are traced through by using carbon paper under the drawing. This only gives a half section. The vertical centre line is traced through as well. The drawing is then turned over, and the vertical centre line laid over the carbon image underneath. The line of the pencil pressing on to the drawing is clear underneath and this is used to draw the other half of the section. Take care that the gunwale line, the deck line, keel line, and the central spine hole are all traced through in place. The exact shape is now outlined on the blockboard. This shape is however too large. Allowance must be made for the thickness of the cladding that will be laid over framework, on top of which will be two layers of glass mat and resin, and on top of that will be thin layers of filler. The whole skin thickness will be about $\frac{3}{8}$-in. Therefore, draw all around inside the section shape traced through, so that the inside line is $\frac{3}{8}$-in. inside the traced line. The spine hole is the same size. The points on the gunwale, keel and deck ridge where the relative stringers go are marked out to take the stringers available. The finished section looks like Fig. 35. The sections are all cut out and numbered in order as they are traced.

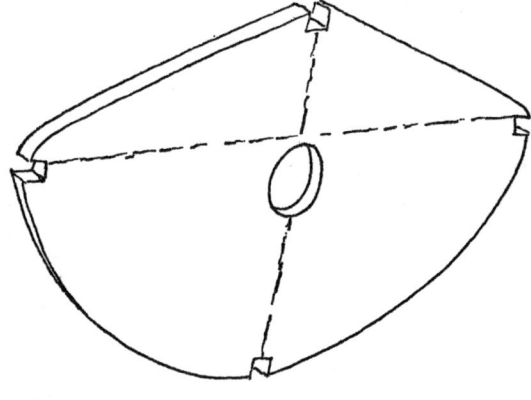

Fig. 35

I once got two sections reversed in a centre section, and didn't spot it until I found odd little ripples in the skin around the centre. That had to be smoothed out with copious quantities of filler, and much time.

The sections are then threaded on to the spine, taking great care about their proper order. It is necessary first to mark off the spine with pencil or felt pen, every 12 in. Because the spine is round in section the sections will turn on it. This is why the stringers are required. Fix the stringers to the centre sections first, and work towards the ends. The last foot at each end is ignored at this stage. When the stringers are fixed, and the overall shape looks right, then cut the stringer ends off about 3 in. beyond the last section.

The spine is rigged on trestles at a convenient working height, and two adjustable slings are fixed under it, as shown in Fig. 36. Look along the end of the tube, through the central hole. It is easy to line up the eye and, say, the top edge of the hole. It will not be possible to see through it as the bend in the tube because of the weight on it will prevent a clear sight straight through. Start taking up the tension in the slings, gently, so as to straighten the tube. Eventually you can look along the inside of the top edge of the tube without hindrance. The lateral straightness of the tube is, or should be, no problem. The

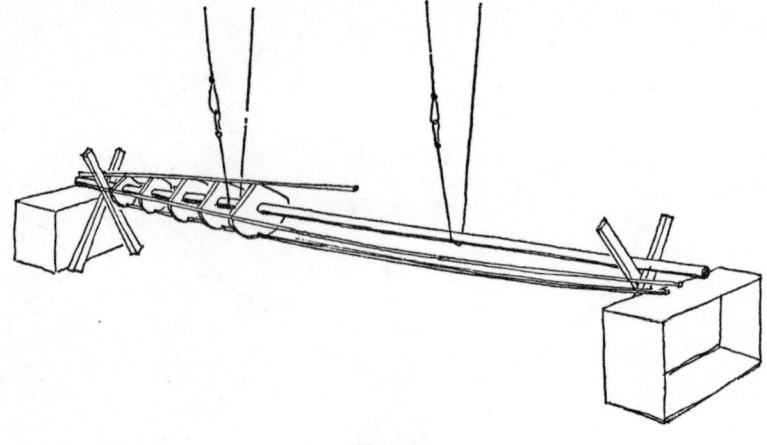

Fig. 36

stringers should accept this slight alteration of attitude without trouble.

Turn the whole skeleton upside down, hull uppermost. Re-rig the suspension cords to include the gunwale stringers. Re-adjust for vertical alignment. Check any 'wind' in the skeleton. Lay sticks across the gunwale stringers at front and back and in the middle and look along. Any twist can be seen, and with the help of an assistant to hold the frame firmly at one end, the other end can be twisted to remove the wind. In Fig. 37 the stern is nearest, and the three winding sticks show a twist from the stern towards the front in an anti-clockwise direction. Leave the winding sticks in place until they finally must be removed.

Take clean sheets of cardboard, and offer them up to the frame, working from the centre towards the ends, alternately stern and bow. Each time a panel is fixed, check the wind. Draw on the underneath of the cardboard where each section is. Allowing for the thickness of the frame, or section, cut out the cardboard panel. It should run across the hull from gunwale to gunwale without break, and between adjacent frames or sections. Take care that it comes to the mid line of the thickness of the frame. Staple into place about every 2 in., working from keel stringer to gunwale. Draw and cut and fit the next

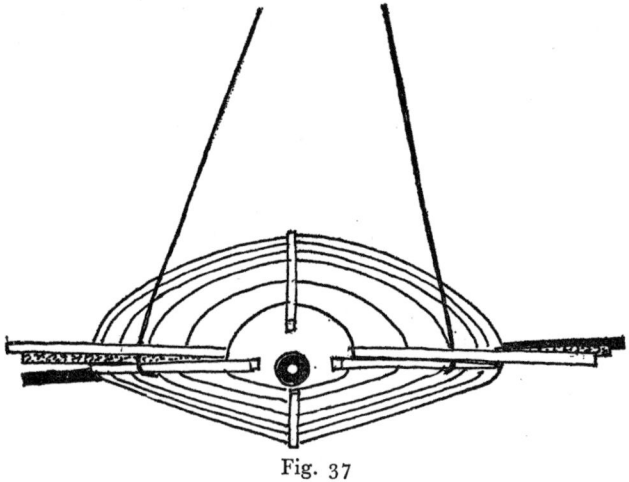

Fig. 37

panel to one side, and fix in the same way. The cardboard panels must be nearly the same thickness, with a butt joint.

When the hull panels are all fitted and stapled in place, during which time it may be necessary to remove one sling at a time, but only after another sling has been fitted to take the strain, then check the wind again. When satisfied, then remove the winding sticks. In fact you must, because the skin of cardboard will ensure that this is done. If there is a twist still in the shell, then it must be completely removed, and re-stapled. At places of tight curvature, it may be necessary to put in staples every half an inch.

Now cut a sheet of chopped strand mat, I used $1\frac{1}{2}$-oz. mat, and lay it on the cardboard shell. Mix up about 4 lb. of resin and paint it all over. Let the resin wet through, and then roll it lightly with a hard roller. If a cardboard panel should come loose and spring up then simply put staples through mat and resin and cardboard. Having put on the first skin, then put on the second skin at once, whilst the first is still wet. I usually find all the scraps of mat and cloth that I may have in the box, and slap it on as carefully as I can when working in a hurry, leaving plenty of overlap where necessary. Wet through, roll down, and leave it alone overnight. You should check the vertical alignment of the spine tube before you leave it, just to make sure it is still right. Once this skin has hardened, there will be no adjustment possible afterwards, except by filling. One final point, if there is a flap of cardboard that simply will not lie down, and it is before the glass and resin goes on, you can use plenty of paper masking tape to cover it over and so tie it down; or you can tie thin string or thread all around the job just to hold it down in place. The string can be put on after the resin has gone on, but paper tape will not stick on resin-wet surfaces.

Next day, turn the canoe over in the slings, trim off the raggy edge which now hangs upwards, and get ready to clad the deck with cardboard. Before you do this, take out any wedges which might hold the spine tube in place, because it comes out after the deck is fixed.

Clad the deck completely with cardboard. You can leave a small rough hole where the cockpit is to go, but don't bother with an accurate fit at this stage. Resin and glass, two layers as before. Smooth the raggy edge over on to the hull skin, do not leave it hanging raggy as before. This ensures a good strong joint, deck to hull. Leave to harden overnight.

Next, get some help, and wrestle the spine tube out of the plug. It helps to thump it with a large mallet, taking care to protect the mallet head with a pad of wood held over the end of the tube. Eventually it starts to move, and soon you can brace your foot against the end section, and pull the tube out. By this time the plug is suspended from two slings only. The end trestles are no longer useful as the tube has gone. You cannot work on a swinging plug, so find something firm for the plug to rest on. Incidentally at this stage, the shape you have is properly called the armature, and is not yet a plug. The whole now weighs about 60 lb.

The ends of the boat now need attention. Obtain some polyurethane foam blocks. You can stick thin sheets together to make blocks, or you can make your own from foaming resin. Just get a large plastic bag, a fair bit larger than the end block you require, put in the necessary amount of mixed resin (About 1/30 the volume you require) and let it foam up inside the bag. After ten minutes you should be able to strip the bag off it. This is then fitted to the stringer stubs and held in place with masking

tape when ready for fixing. Two skins of glass and resin are
formed over the shaped block, with about 2 in. overlap on to
the hull and deck. Whilst this is setting, you can work on the
cockpit hole. Incidentally, do not use polystyrene foam with
polyester resin, because the resin will rot the foam away to a thin
greasy smear. Polystyrene foam and epoxy resin can be used
together. Most people use polyester resin, however.

The cockpit can be a problem if this is your very first attempt
at a plug. Usually I simply take a section of deck from another
canoe, with a cockpit that I wish to use in the new boat, and
graft that deck section into the deck. The important thing to
remember is that all you want is an accurate hole, and of
course it isn't there! Only the bit surrounding it. It is not important how irregular and how badly the section of grafted
deck fails to conform with the plug. Cut out a regular shape,
lay this on the plug, taking very great care to line it up according to the measurements discussed in the section on calculations,
and draw around it. Cut that section out of the deck inside
the line thus drawn. Put the section of deck in place. Stick it
in place with masking tape. Mark off points in pairs, as these
you will drill through with a 3/32 drill bit. One point on the
deck edge, and one on the cockpit rim edge. Take apart and
drill the holes, perhaps 20 or 30 all round. Stitch these together
with bits of wire stripped from old electric wiring, or bits of
nylon fishing line. If any sections of the cockpit rim piece stick

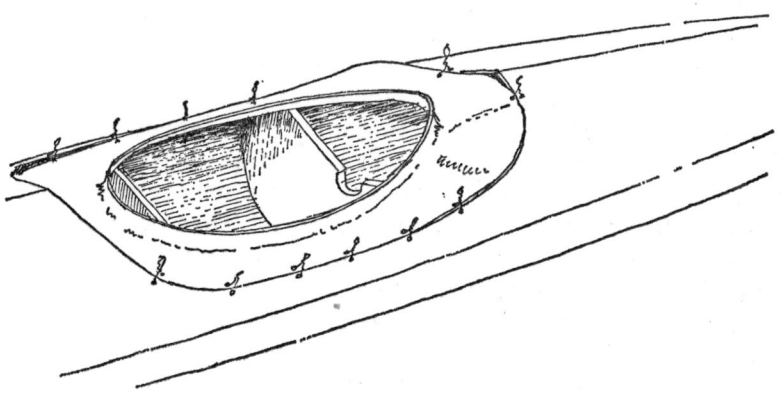

Fig. 38

up above the deck level, do not try to force it down and so distort the cockpit hole. Just fix it in place as it is. Small irregularities can be eased out. Put more holes and stitches in if necessary.

As the hole for the cockpit rim develops, and it becomes necessary to sink some parts of the rim deeper into the deck, it will be necessary to cut away parts of one or two frames. It is probably better to do that at the beginning before the fitting of the cockpit progresses very far. When the rim has been stitched into place, sling the whole canoe upside down about head height. Use rectangles of glass mat, about 3 in. by 6 in., and pre-wetted with gelcoat resin in order to fix the inside of the rim to the inside of the cardboard deck. Make sure these pieces also mould around parts of the frames in order to get a firm hold.

When this is set, the wire ties are pulled off with pliers, or ripped off with a sanding disc.

Once again the plug is set on a firm base at a convenient working height, and work can continue. The ends are roughly formed, the cockpit rim is in place, and the whole hull and deck is nearly the shape required, although with some rough protruding places, such as edges of glass that were not properly stuck down, raised edges around the cockpit, and lumps generally over frames. Take a good sanding disc in a power-drill, and a dust mask and old clothes that you don't mind getting dusty, and rip the surface down as evenly as you can. The best way to do this is to look along the surface of the plug, as though you were looking along the tangent to a drawn curve, and so identify bumps. Hollows of course you can forget about. At this stage you will be cutting down about one-tenth of the surface of the plug. If you go through the two skins of glass and resin, because you absolutely must remove some huge bump, then rip into it with gusto. Shift it! Then open out the hole, perhaps as much as 10 in. by 6 in. This tears out the cardboard and reveals the frame inside. If the cause of the bump is a frame fault, then it is necessary to grind away the edge of the frame until it is down below the profile required. Now depress the edge of the hole a little if you can, and make a piece of cardboard to fit exactly, as an inlay in this hole.

Tape it into position with masking tape. For small holes you can simply cover the hole with strips of masking tape laid edge upon edge until it is covered. Glass over this repair, one layer if the surface is close to the required profile, two layers if there is now a depression in the surface.

Now go all over the plug looking for hollows. It is easier sometimes to do this by stroking the surface with the palm of the hand and feeling where the faults are. Mix up a dough of gelcoat resin and glass mat strands, and be quick with it, as it hardens within ten to fifteen minutes in average temperatures, say 20°C. Use a palette knife, and smear the dough into the hollows, but try to keep all parts of this coarse filler below the profile required. It is simple to fill in the large hollows that this is used; if as a consequence you then have to grind off the surface you have given yourself unnecessary work.

The plug is now roughly the required shape and profile, humps and hollows being no more than a quarter of an inch maximum. Obtain a large tin of filler. I was in the habit of using 'David's Isopon P 38' which is excellent, but expensive compared with the similar but much cheaper filler which most firms which supply resin and glass can supply. I use that which Trylon retails. Find a suitable palette, I use a piece of broken plywood paddle blade, and start mixing. Mix about enough to fill a breakfast cup, and work quickly. Slap it on to the plug, anywhere, say in front of the cockpit, and with the spreader supplied, wipe it as thinly as you can all over the surface. Wipe the palette clean, and wipe the wiper clean, and mix some more. Keep on going until the surface is just about entirely covered with filler. Gritty bits leave streaks in the filler, but ignore them at this stage. If the wiper gets sticky with hardened filler, or if crumbs of it are left on the palette, you will have all kinds of trouble in trying to get a smooth surface. So work clean. (I think that I must put up a sign in the College workshop as follows . . . 'For clean work, work clean.')

As you work onwards the first mix will be hardening enough to cut down. Do the whole foredeck. Leave it and then fill the whole rear deck. Now return to the foredeck and start the very tedious but essential hand work using an Aven 'Millenicut' file, or one of the body files which motor car body workers use, or an old fashioned 'dreadnought' file and cut away at the filler surface and try to remove humps. At this stage you should be cutting down about 40 per cent of the surface. The cut surface looks light, the uncut and the hollow surface looks darker. With these tell-tales to guide you, mix more filler, and fill these darker hollows. Use great care to get it right. Also, try and fill some of the little grooves that dusty particles left in the first application of filler.

Do not at this stage use a cutting disc in a power drill. It will leave its tell-tale circular grooves in the surface, and you will get the rippled surface so typical of the amateur canoe on which not enough time has been spent to get it right. A small orbital sander with a coarse (50 grit) paper can do the job, but I find it rather slow compared with hand cutting. Besides the arm exercise makes me sweat, keeps me fit, and makes my arm strong for paddling (I keep telling myself). Commercial plug makers will use the big industrial orbital sanders with some power in them. The handyman sander lacks power.

When the deck is cut down, turn the job over and tackle the hull. I find that as the surface is bigger it is better to do it in four sections, fore left, fore right, aft left and aft right, going from one section to another allowing time for the filler to harden enough to cut. Start to cut too soon and the still soft filler will clog the file. This can be cleaned out with a wire brush if tackled at once.

When the hull is cut down, turn it on its side and pay attention to the gunwale edge, along which the highlights shine and tend to show up sloppy workmanship. A chap who used to drive a hearse once told me, that when there was a rush on on a muddy winter's day, and he hadn't time to wash it all down before the next funeral, all he did was squirt a hose on the wheels and brush them down; the clean wheels seemed to make the rest look better. For the same reason, keep the lines of the gunwale clean, even if the rest is a bit rippled. It soothes the eye.

Having done both sides with the second coat of filler, return to the deck and the cockpit. It may still be rippled. The next bit calls for some filling and moulding, almost sculpting the rim to a smooth shape. If knee bulges are required, make large blobs of dough and place them where required, or if you can afford lots of filler, make them out of filler. Put them in the right place for the average knee.

When installing knee bulges do remember what their purpose is. There is a drawing in the arrangement of the cockpit section that explains this. Build up with rough lumps, but do not build up above the required profile. It may help to have a cardboard profile both longitudinally and laterally on each bump, held in place with masking tape, and simply filled in each quadrant. Having moulded the cockpit rim into place with filler, start to file it down using the flat Millenicut, and a rat tail engineer's file or better, a half round body file such as motor body workers use. I find that working around the cockpit area takes more time than any other part of the job does. Follow the filing with a second coat of filler around the cockpit, and then file again and start sanding with 50 grit sanding paper, sometimes called 'production paper'. Wrap it around a block of spongy resilient rubber, not soft sponge, but fairly firm. This takes a good curve and spreads the cutting load on the job.

Now for the third and possibly final coat of filler. (This depends on how clever you are.) Sweep out the workshop, clean the bench, remove grit and dust, and clean your tools. Now start to fill the surface, using firm pressure to press out the filler as evenly as possible over as large an area as possible and as thinly as possible. Fill all scratches, cuts, drill holes, etc. Let it harden then rub down with 120 grit paper. Dust off, and coat with Furane resin.

Furane resin is a thin fluid, which air dries in 30 minutes and hardens in two hours, hardening as a resin in 24 hours. It is applied, coat upon coat, without sanding down, until at least four coats and possibly six coats have been applied at intervals of about two hours. (Less than that and you pull the earlier coat off.) The resin has to be mixed, one part of hardener to ten parts of resin. It goes on a dark chocolate colour, then hardens a dense black. It fills all the sanding scars and small cracks.

Twenty-four hours after the last coat has been applied, possibly two days in cold weather, start to rub down the surface with a sanding block with 180 grade wet and dry used wet. Use plenty of rubbing paper. I always cut each sheet into four quarters, so as to economise. I generally use 5 or 6 sheets on each plug. When this has been done all over, and some places are showing the pale grey of the underlying filler through the dense black of the furane surface, dry it off thoroughly, and look at it. You will see that where the surface has been cut down the black is dull and lighter in colour. But where there are hollows, usually cracks, these remain deep black and shiny. Having identified the many little irregularities, mix up tiny amounts of filler, say a teaspoonful at a time, and fill these places with great care. Roughen the shiny surface first to help the filler to stick.

Having gone over the boat end to end with the utmost care, rub down the hardened filler with 360 grade wet and dry used wet on a hard rubbing block. Dry off after sponging down, and when really dry, give it four more coats of furane resin. At this stage you cannot risk smears, so that the deck must be done one day and the next, and the hull the two days after that. When thoroughly hard, cut down the surface lightly with 360 grade wet and dry used wet, followed with 500 or 600 grade wet and dry used wet. Don't worry if you cut through into the filler, but try to keep these patches to a minimum. The slightest hint of lightness where you are rubbing means you must stop at once.

When this has been done, and the whole mopped over and thoroughly dried, then rub over a small area with cutting paste, I use 'T CUT' a proprietary brand for bringing up the shine on old motor cars. It is very like the polish I used to know as Brasso. Polish well by hand. I have used a polishing mop in a drill, but this can rip up the furane surface, and destroy the work of days. I think hand work is better at this stage. I spend a whole day on this stage, polishing and polishing and thinking old thoughts. It's boring and tedious but the shine is worth while.

Incidentally, what sells a canoe is as much shine and bright colour and fancy transfers as good design. Besides, a good shine at this stage lasts for every boat. After the buffing paste has been used, then begins the polishing with wax. It must be a beeswax, never a silicone. Silicone gives a lovely shine, but it links with resin, and when you apply the gelcoat for the mould, it will surely stick. So use wax polish. I prefer 'Mirrorglaze' which is expensive but I like the finish it gives and the smell it has. After the first coat of polish, which must be well done, the shine will begin to appear on the boat, and now you can see all the tiny irregularities which the glossy highlights now begin to show. Don't be unhappy about it, everyone experiences this.

In case you don't know how to apply a coat of polish, it is done as follows.

Take a cloth well soaked with the wax, and make a small rubbing pad to fit into the palm of the hand, held between finger and thumb, with the ball of the thumb and the knuckles to press down. Rub wax on to a small area with a quick smearing motion all over it, say 2 or 3 square feet. Now start rubbing in small circular movements, progressing in swathes about 4 in. across. Wipe lengthways and then sideways. Do the next section, then return to the first and cut down the surface with a clean dry piece of towelling. Leave that area, then apply polish to the third area, return to the second area, and cut that down. Return to the first area and polish that with another dry clean piece of towelling, and buff it up. Polish area 4, cut off area 3, and buff up area 2. Keep this going until the whole boat is done. Leave to harden for at least six hours, then polish in the same way again. It is not good polishing more frequently than that, as the wax must air dry, and it takes six hours. Damp conditions cause trouble. The plug should have at least five coats of wax before moulding can be attempted. I have had some hard luck occasionally with this, using five coats, and have had sticking moulds. That is tragic. Never use a power tool to polish, it simply rips up the wax skin.

If you are in a hurry to have the mould made, then you can take a short cut. In fact I prefer this method as it is safer, but the quality of the finish suffers. A surface that has been built up by repeated polishing with wax will retain a fine gloss and even, in the best work, a mirror-like glitter. However, it is possible to apply one coat of wax and then use one coat of release agent, PVA (poly-vinyl-alchohol). I prefer the coloured PVA as you can see where it has gone. If you apply the PVA immediately after the wax, the PVA will bubble and blob, and will not lie evenly on the job. This is because the wax is still drying out. In that case you can continue to wipe the PVA on, until it becomes so nearly dry that it will smear on and stay in place, without blobbing. Usually I apply PVA with a soft piece of sponge, but sometimes it is better to use a soft brush, not new, a brush in which the loose bristles have already dropped out. Sometimes one can apply the PVA directly to the plug, wait until it is dry, then apply wax, and then another coat of PVA. Or you can apply two good coats of PVA, so that the release agent is fairly thickly spread on the plug. If you use thick layers of PVA, they can form runs as in paint, and these end in blobs of PVA which dry out, the shape of the blob comes through on to the mould, and this appears on the finished job. The danger with using just one thin layer of PVA on a raw plug is that you may not quite cover the whole job with release agent, it only requires one little spot to stick, and this tends to rip out a section of mould, or plug, when releasing of the two is attempted.

Your approach to polishing should be guided by the work you have done so far. If the plug is perfect, then it is well worth while polishing and polishing, putting say eight or ten coats of wax on, before attempting to make the mould. But if the plug surface has faults on it, and the job is fairly rough, and you are in a hurry, then it is worth following the pattern of work as described as far as polishing, putting on the PVA fairly thickly, and taking off the mould. The high quality finish is then worked directly into the mould.

CHAPTER SEVEN

Making the Mould

The canoe or kayak shell is a closed object, with a cockpit hole. The method is to use moulds to make the deck and hull separately, then the two moulds are used as jigs which hold the two parts together whilst the joint is made, working through the cockpit hole. Some firms prefer to cast the two parts in the moulds, then to remove them from the moulds and join them outside the moulds. This is better in some ways, and not so good in others.

In order to make the two halves of the moulds, it is necessary to make a flange all around the widest part of the canoe. In the case of a normal boat, that is along the gunwale line. In the case of, say, a surf-shoe, the line of the joint would be along the 'rail' where the side turns sharply into the bottom, which is flat. In any event, imagine a mould for a wine bottle. If the opening through which the cast must be withdrawn is less in size than the widest diameter of the bottle, it will simply not come out. However, in the case of canoe, it is possible to make a slightly bottle shaped mould, provided that one end can easily be released. Then, using the flexibility of the mould, the rest can be sprung loose. Mind it can be a dangerous project, for if you get it wrong you are stuck with an immovable object, and irresistible force will simply break it to pieces.

The flange is simply made by making sections of hardboard, or thin plywood, to fit along the widest part of the plug. These flanges can be held in place by slips of alloy, or even stuck on with masking tape and blobs of plasticene. The method of making these temporary flanges is described now.

First of all it is necessary to establish where the joint line is to run. This is done by pulling a long strip of masking tape along the side of the boat, so that the top edge of the tape represents the line of the joint. To get this on dead straight, fix the free end of the tape to one end of the boat, right on the line required, and unreel about half a boat's length of tape. Pull it gently and look along it, with the eye just over the reel. Ease it towards the plug so that it begins to lie along the curve of the joint, always keeping plenty of free tape between the point where the tape is touching the plug and the reel. If the line seems faulty, ease the tape away from the plug, simply by lifting the reel away from it, and re-lay the tape. As the point of attachment of the tape begins to move towards the reel, unreel a little more tape, and so advance the job until you have reached the other end. Break off the tape, and then look at the line you have. If it is dead true, that is fine, simply press the top edge lightly into place with the fingers. If it shows slight kinks along it, then you must undo the tape, and go back to where the kink is, and correct it. Do not press the tape firmly into place until the whole thing lies properly in place.

Make some alloy tabs, about 2 in. by 4 in., or 1 in. by 3 in. These should be fairly stiff, but easily bent into an angle. Bits of old 1 gallon oil cans do just as well. Make about 40 tabs, and drill a small hole in them, just one, a little below centre. Go right round the plug and mark off on the joint line tape

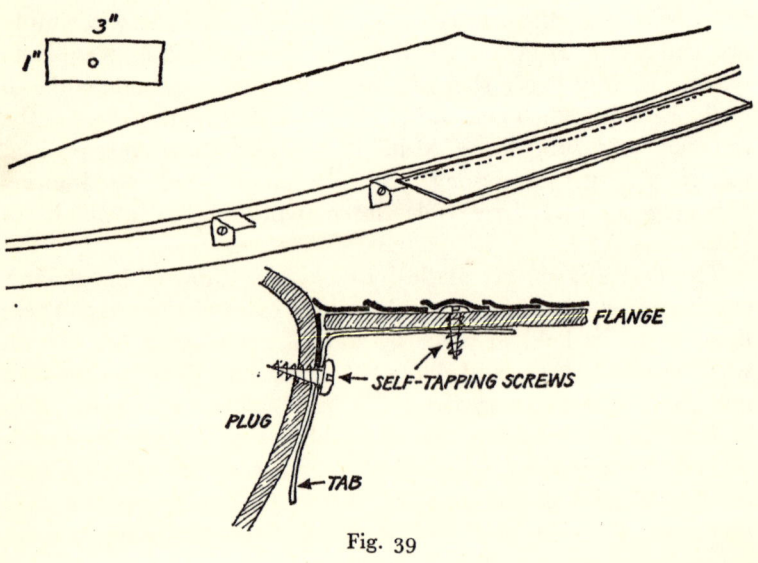

Fig. 39

at 9 or 10-in. intervals. If the material for the flange is fairly
strong and rigid, the tabs can be set further apart. Now drill
straight into the plug, using a bit which is the right tapping
size for self-tapping screws which are used to fix the tabs to the
plug. The holes should be just on, or just under the lower edge
of the tape, where the marks are. Now screw on the flat tabs,
fairly tightly, with the longer end of the tab uppermost. Decide what thickness the flange pieces are to be, and then go all
round the tabs bending them down at right angles to the plug,
using a straight edge to bend them over.

Having fitted all the tabs, then cut some hardboard into
strips 4 ft. long and about 4 to 5 in. wide. Offer them up one
at a time to the plug, resting them on the tabs. Draw a curve
on the top surface of the flange piece parallel to the curve of

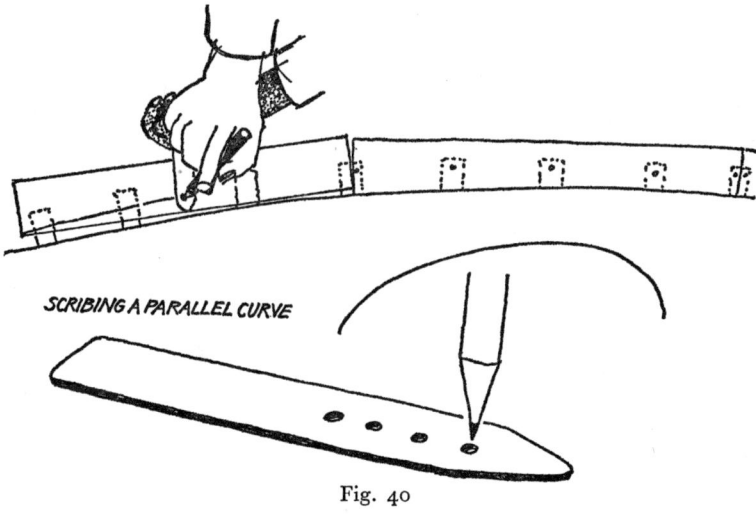

SCRIBING A PARALLEL CURVE

Fig. 40

the plug. Cut out this curve with a coping saw, and hold the
flange piece in place whilst a drill is put through the flange
and the tabs underneath. Screw the flange down to the tab
with another self-tapping screw. Keep on going all round, and
make the joints between flange pieces along the width of the
tabs, as this keeps the flange pieces all in the same plane. You
will find that it is not possible to get the flange pieces to fit
dead flush to the plug. I find it easier to cover this slight gap

with masking tape with just a tiny edge on to the plug, and the majority of the tape on the flange. The flange finish is not important, but any intrusion on the plug will affect the mould, and this will affect each subsequent cast. Still, on the finished canoe, the usual joint strip will cover any slight irregularity here. Joints between flange sections are covered with tape, and I prefer to cover the whole flange surface with strips of tape laid edge to edge. This at least gives a fairly smooth surface to the flange, which allows the use of rough surfaced materials for the flange, such as the rough side of hardboard. The tape also covers the screw heads, thus preventing them from being filled with resin and thus becoming useless for further work. Another point is that I always work with the deck uppermost when fixing flanges in this way, the first half of the mould being the deck.

(If you have no experience of laminating glass and resin, it will be helpful at this point to read 'workshop preparations' page 99.)

Having attached the flange all the way around, then prepare the deck for taking off the mould. The surface is either highly polished, as described, or it is now given a coat of release agent, all over the deck, and the flange. Make sure the sealing strip around the flange edge between plug and flange is tightly pressed down, because once the release agent is applied, the tape will not stick. When the release agent is dry, apply the gelcoat, clear, about $1\frac{1}{2}$ lb. for the deck.

When the gelcoat is hard, about 2 hours in normal workshop temperatures, i.e., about 65°F. (20°C.), then laminate the mould as follows. (The way in which lamination is done is described in the section which deals with canoe construction.)

Cut out 42 or 44 strips of mat, 3 in. wide, and 3 ft. long. Cut out two complete sheets of mat, to cover the plug and flange, from flange edge to flange edge. This gives two of the three laminations. The third lamination is of offcuts and bits and pieces from the scrap box.

Mix 4 lb. of laminating resin. Brush this quickly all round the flange, simply by walking all round the job and slopping on the resin with a 2-in. brush. Continue circling, only this time lay strips of glass mat on the flange, inner edge just touch-

MOULD LAMINATION STAGES

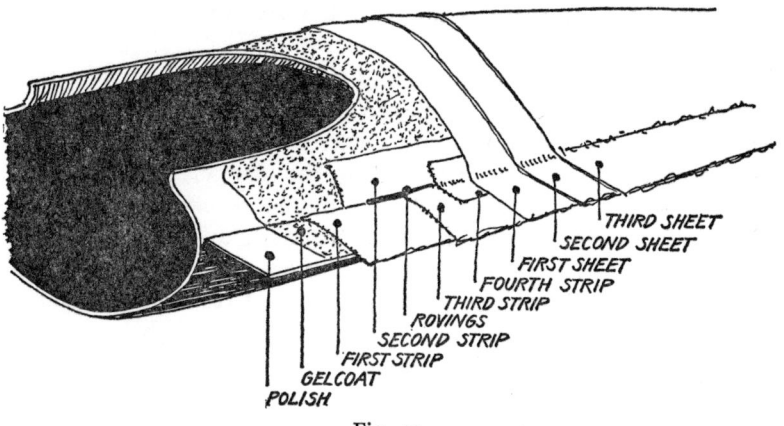

THIRD SHEET
SECOND SHEET
FIRST SHEET
FOURTH STRIP
THIRD STRIP
ROVINGS
SECOND STRIP
FIRST STRIP
GELCOAT
POLISH

Fig. 41

ing the plug, joined edge to edge without overlaps. Complete
the first layer in this way.

Go round the job again, this time slopping resin on to the
deck along a strip about 4 in. wide above the joint line. Lay
strips of glass along this deck piece, as for the flange. Go all
round and paint the surface liberally with resin. Now take a roll
of rovings, and go round the job three times with this long
strand of material, to give a three thickness strand which lies
right in the edge between flange and deck, thus giving strength
to what would otherwise be a weak part.

By now the first layer of glass should have wetted through.
There will be bubbles trapped under it. It has not yet wetted
out. The second layer of glass strip goes on to the flange. No
more resin should be required. Now go right round the job
using a small diameter ribbed roller so as to squeeze out all the
entrapped air. The last strip of glass is used to span the gap
between the two horizontal strips on the flange and the single
strip on the deck. More resin will be required, and great care
should be taken to smooth down the upper edge of the strip,
where it lies against the deck surface. This edge must be in-
distinct.

The 4 lb. of resin should now be about finished. There may
be enough to laminate two thicknesses of glass strip around the

edge of the cockpit hole, in order to give it some extra thickness just here. If there is no resin left this thickening can be left until last.

Mix up about 5 lb. of resin, and using a soft roller, cover the whole deck with resin. Lay on the first layer of mat, and again cover this with resin from the roller, using it liberally. It will be necessary to use a brush along the flange. Roll all over quickly with a hard roller, then lay on the second layer. Cover again with resin, mixing more if required, and roll down as before. Now use strips of offcuts, and so on, and cover the whole job as quickly as possible, as the first mix of resin will be going off. Three laminations of $1\frac{1}{2}$-oz. mat should be enough. Thicken the edges of the cockpit hole, and where these are deeply recessed, it is useful to mix up a dough of resin and glass mat bits, and lay this dough in the recess right up to the cockpit edge. There should be a slight, say 1 in., waste edge sticking up all round the cockpit opening, which will later be trimmed off.

When the deck half-mould is hard, then draw a line all round the flange, using a felt pen, so that the line is about 3 in. from the edge of the deck. Go round this with a jig saw and trim it off, right through everything. Turn the plug over and take out the screws which are used to fix the tabs to the plug. Lever off the flange pieces, taking care not to spring the mould away from the plug. Strip off the paper tape as cleanly as you can from the flange and plug. It is important to get this really neatly done. You may find that the surface under the paper tape is a little sticky, but this will dry out in an hour or two.

Dust any bits off the hull and flange, cover with release agent, and cover with gelcoat. When dry, laminate as for the deck.

When the hull lamination is hard, it can then be trimmed as for the deck flange. However, if you are quick, you can catch the laminate when it is green, and trim it with a sharp knife. This saves a bit of work later on.

Now go all round the rough edge of the flange with a sanding disc and give it a smooth edge. Mark off every foot or so on the flange, and drill holes through both flanges, using a $\frac{5}{32}$ drill bit, about 1 in. from the inner edge of the flange. The

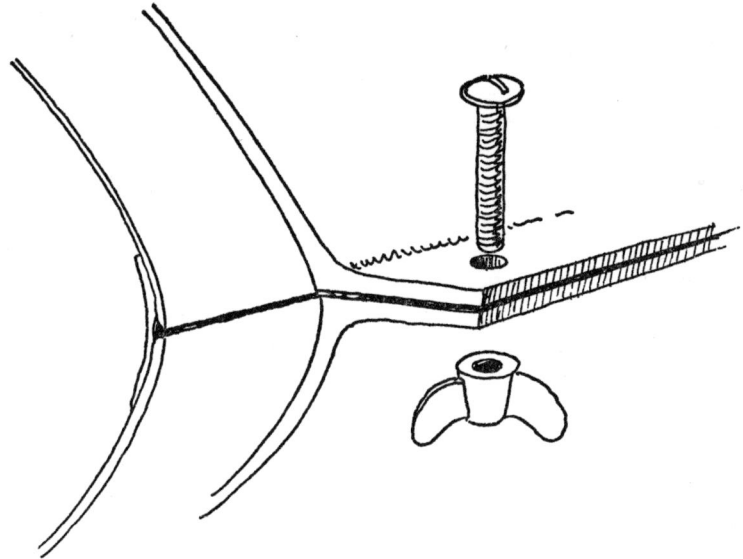

Fig. 42

cockpit opening should also be trimmed clean and sanded level with the plug. Some mould makers leave a highstanding flange here, which makes a canoe where the cockpit hole has to be enlarged before the cockpit can be fitted. This is to leave plenty of spare material around the mould to allow for wear later.

The moulds are now separated by levering the flange apart with a 3-in. or 4-in. bricklayer's bolster. Slide this along the flange levering both up and down. The air can be seen slipping between the plug and the mould as you go along. If you cannot see it, you may well have a sticking mould, which is a very nasty experience, and it means that your releasing preparations have not been adequate. The separation does require a fair bit of effort, and help is useful. The deck usually comes off first. Lay it aside. Place the hull on the ground, and stand in the cockpit on one foot. You may not be able to do this with a new plug as the internal structure may prevent this. Thrust downwards with the foot against one flange, and then against the other. They should separate from the plug along the edge with a crack. Stand astride the plug, and by bracing both hands down upon the flanges, thrust downwards, to continue

D

the separation along the edge. At the very ends lay a piece of strong wood across the flange end, and then strike the piece of wood with a mallet, fairly firmly but not heavily. This should jolt the end of the canoe free in the mould. Do this at each end. Turn the mould over and see if it is clear and separate all along. When it is, lift it out and set it aside.

The plug should be kept safe for a few weeks until the first few canoes have been made, just in case something terrible happens to the mould, and the job has to be done again. After that it isn't likely to be much use, as it is heavy and fragile. Commercial plugs for producing moulds are heavy grp castings taken from the moulds.

The moulds are now ready for polishing. First, wash out any trace of release agent. Dry it thoroughly. Wax polish as described, including the flanges. Polish at least three times, then use release agent, and make the first boat. When this is done, wash out the moulds, polish twice again, use release agent, and turn out another boat. Wash out, polish once again, use release agent, and turn out another boat. Wash out.

By this stage, the mould is developing a skin of wax. It may not be particularly well polished however. You can either continue with this system, a coat of wax, and then make a boat, no longer using release agent, or you can cut the surface down, using 'T CUT' and start to develop a really high shine. The wax polishing must be done again, *three* coats in proper order, and then a boat taken out of the moulds, another coat of wax, another boat, until it has about 6 to 8 coats of wax. It should then be possible to take out several boats before polishing again. As soon as the canoes show signs of being sticky to remove from the moulds, then polish once again with wax. After a lot of wax has been put on the mould, there tends to build up a rough skin of wax, which is almost as hard as resin, and which must be cut down with cutting paste, such as 'T CUT'. Any dullness of the surface which cannot be removed by polishing the wax implies wax build-up, and so cutting paste must be used, and a general re-polishing of the moulds. It is of interest that the first polishing takes more wax than subsequent polishings, as the resin is still active, taking something like six weeks to settle down.

CHAPTER EIGHT

Building a Glass Reinforced Plastic Canoe

There are many schools, youth groups, and so on who have experience of building canoes. This section is written for those who have no experience at all. But it is based on my latest working method which I find an improvement on anything I have done before. For example I have laminated a seat and cockpit in 14 minutes compared with the 25 minutes I usually take, and the hour that I used to need for this job. Joining a BAT Mk 8 takes me 25 minutes, both sides done within that time; it used to take me over an hour to do one side. The point I am making is that although this section is aimed at the novice, do read it if you have some experience; you could find just one clue that will reduce your building time by an hour or two.

The main parts of the job are :
    (a)   Setting up the workshop and moulds and materials.
    (b)   Gelcoating the moulds. Cutting the glass.
    (c)   Laminating the parts, and trimming them.
    (d)   Joining hull and deck, cockpit to deck.
    (e)   Finishing off. Rigging deck lines, footrest, etc.

Its true that safety is a state of mind. It is also true that workshop practice is a product either of long experience or firm discipline. I would like you to fix in your minds and follow if you can, these ideas. They really are important.

> *'Cultivate a sense of urgency without haste.'*
> *'Clean work is produced in clean workshops.'*
> *'Time, tide, and setting resin wait for no man.'*

Workshop preparations
There are many ways of organising a workshop, but I will make this as basic as I can. This is what you need.

1. A room as long as the moulds plus 6 ft., about 12 ft. wide, and about 8 ft. high.
2. A bench or trestles on which to rest the moulds at a convenient working height. (Bench top about 30 in. high.)
3. Slings to rig the moulds at shoulder height, suspended from ceiling.
4. A surface on which to cut the chopped strand mat. 6 ft. by 4 ft.
5. A surface on which to mix the resin. 3 ft. by 4 ft.
6. A source of water to wash off splashes of chemicals, etc.
7. A bin in which to put rubbish. A large cardboard box will do.
8. Something to put out fires. Little aerosol cans are no good. Best are powder extinguishers which are at least 4 lb. size. The novice with limited resources should borrow one or two, or at least have some buckets of sand or earth available. Water is not good, it spreads acetone fire like petrol.
9. Ready access to the open air.
10. Tools (Fig. 43).

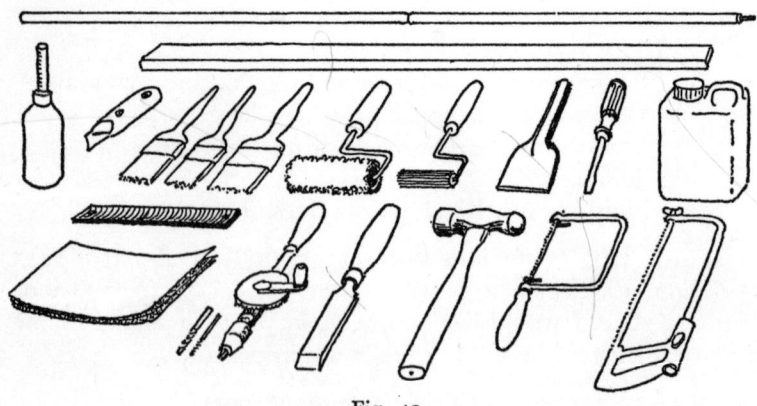

Fig. 43

Knife. Stanley trimming knife, 2 or 3 spare blades.
Straight-edge $3\frac{1}{2}$-ft. long.
Brushes. 2 x 2 in., 1 x 3 in.
Rollers soft and hard. Soft, lambswool, 5 in.; hard ribbed, 3 in.

Catalyst measuring bottle.
Wide bladed lever, like bricklayer's bolster. 3 in. or 4 in.
Screwdriver.
Alloy tent pole about 5 ft. long. (Longer for long canoe.)
Mixing pots. 1-gallon size, polythene.
Coarse file, sandpaper, wet and dry paper.
Hand drill and bit ($\frac{5}{16}$).
Wide bladed chisel (Firmer, 1 in.) slightly blunted.
Hammer.
Coping saw and spare blades.
Hacksaw.
Some large bits of cardboard.
Sheet of window glass, 15 in. by 6 in.

11. Materials.
Chopped strand mat, $1\frac{1}{2}$-oz. (450 gsm) 36 in. wide, 22 yards.
(This is for a 14 ft. by 24 in. beam boat. Others may require more or less.)

Laminating resin. (lay-up resin)	30 lb.
Gelcoat resin	5 lb.
Catalyst, MEKP, liquid	1 lb.
Acetone. (brush cleaner)	4 pints
Colour paste	$\frac{1}{2}$ lb.
Polishing wax	$\frac{1}{4}$ lb.
Barrier Cream	1 lb.
Cleansing cream	1 lb.

Two slabs of polystyrene foam, 1 ft. by 3 ft. by 4 in. One piece
of alloy tube, like tent pole or paddle shaft, 20 in. long approx.,
1 in. dia. approx., 12 gauge.
NB. The quantities of resin and glass are rather over what is
required, but the spare is useful for wastage, and for repair
work later. 'Trylon' provide a useful breakdown of quantities
for 1, 2, 3 or 6 boats. Clearly there are economies in building
a large number of boats. (For suppliers *see* Appendix 2.)

SERIOUS WARNING
This section has been written as simply as possible so that people
without much in the way of workshop resources can see that the
work *is* possible.

Do not ever underestimate the fiery nature of acetone. Flash fires and explosions are quite possible in your garden shed, so *no naked lights*.

Preparation

Lay the hull mould upside down on a bench or on the ground. Cut a length of chopped strand mat just as long as the mould. Lay this over the upturned mould, and make sure that one long edge just meets the edge where the flange starts. There may be a bit of spare material on the other side. Cut all around the mould, pressing the knife blade down on to the outer surface of the mould where the flange turns into the

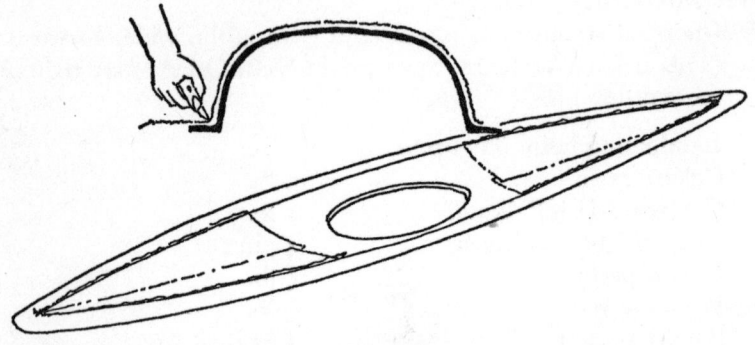

Fig. 44

mould shell. Cut a notch in the bow end of this sheet, so as to identify it. The notch, or slit, is about 6 in. long. Lay the spare material to one side, carefully folded. Cut the second piece like the first. Roll up the two pieces now ready for laminating, and lay them in a clean place. Do not cut the pieces more than a few hours before the job, or dampness may get at the binder which then softens, and the sheets of glass become fluffy and difficult to handle.

Take the spare glass to the deck mould and piece them into the deck. There should be enough from the hull pieces to cover one lamination of the deck. The rest required can be obtained from a piece about two thirds the length of the deck, cut from the unused glass. The deck consists of two layers of $1\frac{1}{2}$-oz. mat all over, with a bridge of strength just in front of the cockpit where a third layer goes, running from the front of the cockpit hole forward for at least 2 ft., but not more than $2\frac{1}{2}$ ft. Carefully take all the pieces of glass and lay them aside in order, so that you can re-assemble them on the mould when laminating begins. It should go without saying that you never cut down on to the polished surface of the mould.

Now, having cut the glass, and laid it aside, you can polish the mould. (*See* notes on polishing.) Apply wax also to the flanges, but no need to polish them. It may seem daft, but I have seen people of some intelligence starting happily to polish the rough side of the mould. It is the smooth side only which should be polished.

The seat mould can now be prepared. You need four strips, wide enough to cover the seat portion from front to back, and long enough to run right across the seat from the edge of one side of the rim to the edge of the other rim. Also, you will need enough strips of glass mat, about 3 in. wide, to cover the rest of the rim four times. The seat is now polished after the glass has been carefully set aside.

Set the deck and hull moulds at a convenient (hip-high) working height. Mix some gelcoat resin in a pot. You need a stick for stirring, and a 3 in. brush, well rubbed to rid it of

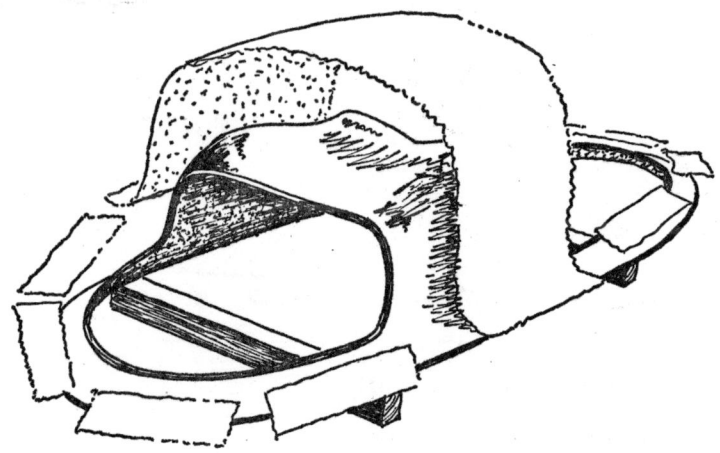

Fig. 45

loose bristles. Gelcoat the hull first, in order to get some idea of the quantity of colour paste that will do the job best. Colour faults do not look so bad on the hull as on the deck. Pour about 2 lb. of gelcoat resin into the pot, add about a dessert-spoonful of colour paste, and stir well together. Now measure out 15–20 ml. of catalyst, and stir this in. Do not add less than this, as there is a basic minimum below which you cannot go without spoiling the job. Now stir slowly and with great care until the catalyst is absorbed into the resin. If you stir vigorously too soon, or add resin to catalyst, neat catalyst can fly up into your eyes and this must AT ONCE be washed out of the eye, or off the skin, because severe chemical burns will begin to hurt you inside ten seconds. Wash it off within that time and you will be all right.

Once the gelcoat resin is thoroughly stirred, which takes time as it is so thick, then start to cover the polished mould surface with it. The idea is to get the resin out of the pot on to the job, so don't wipe surplus amounts off on the edge of the pot or it will take you all day to do it. Use the 3-in. brush and use it as a sort of flat scoop to slop dollops of resin out of the pot

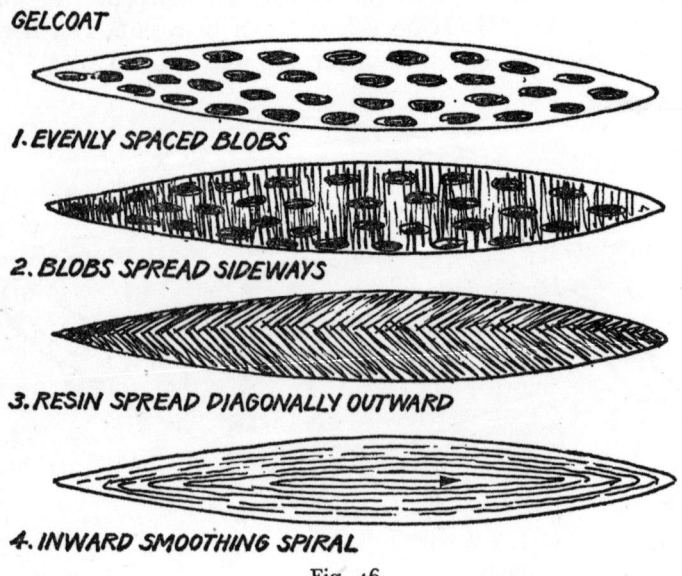

GELCOAT

1. EVENLY SPACED BLOBS

2. BLOBS SPREAD SIDEWAYS

3. RESIN SPREAD DIAGONALLY OUTWARD

4. INWARD SMOOTHING SPIRAL

Fig. 46

on to the mould. Slop it out in streaks, one right at the end, two side by side a bit further along, then three side by side next, as the mould widens, then four streaks side by side at the widest part, the middle part of the boat usually. Slopping on these streaks of resin should take less then five minutes, end to end.

Leave a little spare resin in the pot, and then go back to the beginning. Using the brush as a sort of squeegee, wipe the resin quite roughly from side to side of the mould, from flange to flange, but without putting any resin on the flange, as far as possible. Its like mowing a lawn, you progress steadily, each run across the mould being alongside and edge to edge with the previous run. If there are still some uncovered areas, do not bother, just concentrate on keeping going from one end to the other as quickly as possible. If you find yourself working away at some patch, apply a quick kick to your own posterior, and move on.

Having arrived at the far end, this being the second trip along the mould, start with the brush in the centre of the mould, and about a foot from the end. Angle the brush stroke up, at about 45° to the centre line, to the flange edge. Go along as before, doing half the boat at a time, it being easier to do the side opposite to that on which you are standing. Then come back along the other side, middle diagonally to the edge, spreading upwards from centre to edge. Now walk right round the mould, using the brush along the top edge opposite, ensuring that the top edge is properly covered with resin, and evenly, too. This is where you might use up the last brushful or two that may be still in the pot. Don't waste any. Now walk around and around the mould, starting with the brush along the top edge opposite, and without once stopping or lifting the brush off, complete a spiral inwards as you go around and around the mould, eventually finishing off with a single strip right up the centre, end to end. If you stop walking, or stop the brush, you will get a slight smear, which does spoil the colour job sometimes, especially on white laminates.

Do the deck in the same way. You may have to clean your brush between one job and the other if you are slow, or if the workshop is hot. Mix up about 1½ lb. of gelcoat resin as before, and spread it on as before.

Sometimes it is found that the gelcoat resin has not set. There can be several reasons for this, but the almost certain fact will be that no catalyst has been put in. If, after two or three hours the surface is still wet, you can be assured that you have forgotten the catalyst. Check in several places, just to make sure. There are two ways to tackle this problem, either strip it out with rags and acetone, or give it a 'catalyst cocktail'. This is a high energy, high risk mixture, should it be anywhere near to a naked light, so do take care.

Take about 200 ml. of acetone and add to it about 100 ml. of catalyst. Stir gently with a clean brush, then brush lightly all over the wet surface. The acetone dries out within a few minutes, and it leaves the catalyst evenly dispersed across the surface. This now starts to leach down into the wet resin, and hardening begins within an hour or so. Once started it gathers speed, and laminating can start quite soon.

Clean the brush by wiping it across the edge of the resin pot repeatedly. Milk the spare resin out of it as much as you can. Fill about half a pint of acetone into a pot, and slop the brush about inside it. You must milk the resin out of the roots of the brush, and the best way to do that is to use the fingers. I work with bare hands, but with barrier cream on. Some people are rather sensitive to the acetone, and must be protected with gloves as well. One book on safety that I have seen, *University of Bath Safety Handbook* states (p. 16) '... acetone ... promotes excessive dryness of the skin ... favourable to dermatitis infection ... and in some cases have carcinogenic properties ...' It also mentioned a number of other solvents like diesel oil, so I don't know if acetone is also a carcinogen. I've been using it for 15 years now, and it hasn't done me any noticeable harm; but people vary in their reaction to such strong solvents. It certainly stings like mad when it gets into skin abrasions, but it doesn't last more than half a minute. It seems to cauterise the wound. My skin lesions seem to heal quickly enough.

Take a 2-in. brush, again rub it well to remove loose bristles, and then mix up a tiny quantity of gelcoat to cover the seat. I find that five or six brush loads of gelcoat resin, lifted out of the container with a clean brush used like a scoop, is just about right. Mix about a mustard spoonful of colour paste into it, and add about 2 ml. of catalyst, stir well, then apply evenly to the seat mould. If you want a different colour for the seat, and you have only one tin of colour paste for the whole job, you can add tiny quantities of good house paint, oil based, and this can do the job. But do take care, I have turned such a mix into a Quatermass-type of jelly that heaved and bubbled and slid off the mould in wriggling lumps, quite fascinating to watch, and wasteful too. If you find a few loose bristles in the gelcoat, either leave them and ignore them, or use the edge of the bristles on the brush to lift them out. You can see loose bristles about to leave the brush if you keep an eye open for them, and then you simply wipe them off on a handy piece of cardboard.

Now that the moulds are gelcoated, you can leave them for about two hours, before they will be ready for laminating. Try not to let anything drop into the moulds at this stage, such as little bits of rubbish, water drips from shed roofs in the wet, flies (which seem to like the stench of setting resin . . . I do too, come to that), and odd chips of resin and crumby bits of partially-set resin. Even if you put a sheet of polythene over the moulds to keep off rubbish, I have seen such sheets drop in their own quota of bits, hidden in folds, or drop into the mould themselves where they cling lovingly to the gelcoat, thus ruining the job. If it is a nice hot sunny day, you can turn the moulds upside down and put them on the ground in a sunny patch, where they will go off in fifteen minutes.

During this waiting time you should prepare the odds and ends. You will need a hull stiffener, and I usually make my own stiffener former by laminating one layer of mat into a piece of angle alloy, well waxed, at least 1 in. across the angle, and about 12 ft. long. Or you can buy a 12 ft. long piece of wooden 'D' moulding from the handyman shop and laminate that in. If you are making your own, mix up about a cupful of laminating resin, cut four strips of glass mat each $1\frac{1}{2}$ in. wide from the width of the glass, and lay these into the hollow side of the angle material, making a slight overlap joint at each joint of the four strips. The method is to go along from one end to the other, and lay the glass strips over the open side of the alloy mould. It may help to wedge the mould upright by making blobs of plasticene, or cutting wedge shapes out of small blocks of foam plastic, or out of wood, and so supporting the alloy. Having laid the strips on, paint from end to end, quite quickly, with the resin. Go back to the beginning, and press the glass into the mould with the brush. Go back to the start again, and again press the glass down, ensuring that the glass is completely wetted through with resin. Leave it to harden. This is a useful exercise in seeing how resin and glass work, to see how resin takes time to wet through the glass, as the binder softens.

You may be fitting a footrest too, this is advisable for a personal boat, but canoes which are to be used by many novices often lose their footbars, and they can be a nuisance, so I don't bother to fit footrests to that sort of boat. However, if you do, obtain a piece of window glass about 15 in. by 6 in., and rub it with wax. Resin can stick to glass strongly enough to rip out small pieces from a sheet of glass. Cut four strips of glass mat, each about 12 in. by 5 in., and mix up about a cupful of laminating resin and 4 ml. of catalyst. Using a 2-in. brush, lay resin on the waxed glass, lay on the first piece of glass mat, brush on more resin, then the next piece of glass mat, until all four pieces of glass mat are laminated one upon the other. Now use the hard roller, and squeeze the air bubbles out of the job. Leave this piece of work to harden. Clean the brush and the roller most carefully.

Laminating process

Ensure gelcoat is hard enough. Touch the edge with your finger tip. If it feels slightly sticky, not wet, and if no colour lifts off on your finger tip, then it is ready. Touch the gelcoat in various places all over, to ensure it has hardened all over.

Mix up about 5 lb. of laminating resin with about a dessert-spoonful of colour. You need less colour paste in the laminating resin than you do in the surface gelcoat. Stir in about 35 ml. of catalyst. Stir thoroughly, and carefully, but as the laminating resin is more runny than the gelcoat it mixes more easily. Use the soft roller, and slop resin on to the gelcoat in the mould. Use the roller like a scoop at this stage, just pulling out great blobs of resin on to the job. Now roll the resin out, generously, on to the surface. You should have used about half the 5 lb. mix.

Lay in the first layer of glass, slit end to the front. Ease the glass mat into place by hand, starting centrally, moving towards the ends, pulling the mat sideways so that it lies dead centre in the mould. This must be done before pressing the mat down on to the resin, and it must be done quickly so that the mat can be pressed down on to the resin before it runs down to the bottom of the mould. Having placed it fairly well by hand, quickly roll all over with a dryish soft roller so that the resin underneath starts to come through. Put resin into the ends by using the brush.

Now slop on more resin, and this should nearly use up what you have in the pot. Ensure that all the glass is covered with resin, especially the top edges of the cast. There should be a waste edge of about $\frac{1}{4}$-in. all round at this stage. Spend a few minutes, say five, consolidating the job using the soft roller and brush. Mix up some more resin, 4 lb. this time. Lay in the second layer of glass, and press into place and wet with resin as before. Not more than fifteen minutes should have passed by now. Having once again ensured that the entire surface is covered with resin, start using the hard roller, and very methodically cover the whole job, rolling steadily but not fast. The whistle and thrash of a roller moving at high speed is the sound associated with someone who is dedicated to putting resin on the ceiling and passing friends as it flies off the spinning roller. Apart from which the roller does not stay in one place long enough to squeeze out the air bubbles, which is what its purpose it. I find that if I start at one end in the middle, roll from where the bottom turns up into the side, right across the bottom from side to side, then roll upwards from the bottom to the top edges of the sides, and finally all around the top edge with the roller held vertically, I get a good, steady, methodical coverage.

Now take a brush and paint the rest of the resin all around the top edge of the job, let it drain down how it will. Any dry spots anywhere else, then slop more resin on to them. Finally, go all over with the soft roller again, and the hard roller if there is time. .

Now cut some pieces of glass, actually I use the long triangular pieces left over when the deck material was pieced together, and these should be about 3 in. by 18 in. These are laminated into the ends of the canoe, lengthways along the keel. They are simply thickeners to increase wear resistance. One layer should do, but you can use two layers if you like.

Lay the stiffener former into the hull, lengthways along the keel, it does not necessarily have to be in one piece, and cut four pieces of glass mat, each 4 in. wide by 3 ft. long, and lay these end to end over the stiffener former. Paint the surface with resin. You may have to mix a little more resin for this. Go quickly from end to end. The joints should overlap about half an inch. Roll with the hard roller. Brush all over again ensuring that resin is on all the glass and roll again. Use the brush lightly and quickly to scuff up the surface of the glass along the edges of the stiffener, and then press it down smoothly. This gives a smooth edge to it. The hard cut edge should now be moulded into the surrounding laminates and be almost invisible. If you can see a hard straight edge to the stiffener strip, it is not so well laminated as if the edge were moulded into the surrounding laminates. Any hard and sharp edge in a load-carrying structure will concentrate stresses, cracks and structural failure will start at these places.

The deck is laminated in the same way. The tools are all cleaned before the deck lamination is done. It is also good practice to clean out the pot too, as after a while, say an hour, bits of resin still in the pot from the first mix are starting to gel, and this action starts off succeeding mixes of resin. This can spoil quite large mixes of resin. When you do clean it, do it thoroughly.

Start as before, by mixing 5 lb. of resin, and wetting all the deck. Lay in the first lamination, being sure that it is the lamination with the biggest pieces in it. Be particularly careful to poke the resin and glass at the very ends into the end, using a brush to do it. Make sure that the edges of the glass that drape over the edge of the cockpit rim are thoroughly wetted. Try not to get a waste edge of more than half an inch at any point. Put in the second layer for the deck, then put in the bridge of strength in front of the cockpit, where there are three laminations. This is where rescue work will cause the deck to be subjected to considerable strain. You will probably find that the 5 lb. of resin will just about do the whole job, but if it doesn't, mix up another 1 or s lb. Clean all tools very carefully.

Now you must fit the footrest flanges. Take the four-laminate sheet, and separate it from the sheet of glass. Clean the glass and set it aside. Mark off the footrest flanges as shown. Cut out using a coping saw, or even an ordinary saw with fine teeth. A hacksaw will do as well. Mount face to face in a vice, and file the edges clean and smooth. Remember your feet may be rubbing against the edge for hours on a long trip, and they can become very sore if up against a rough edge. Drill holes parallel to the edges that will be facing inwards, about $\frac{3}{4}$-in. in from the edge and about $1\frac{1}{2}$ in. apart. Rub the filed edges with sandpaper.

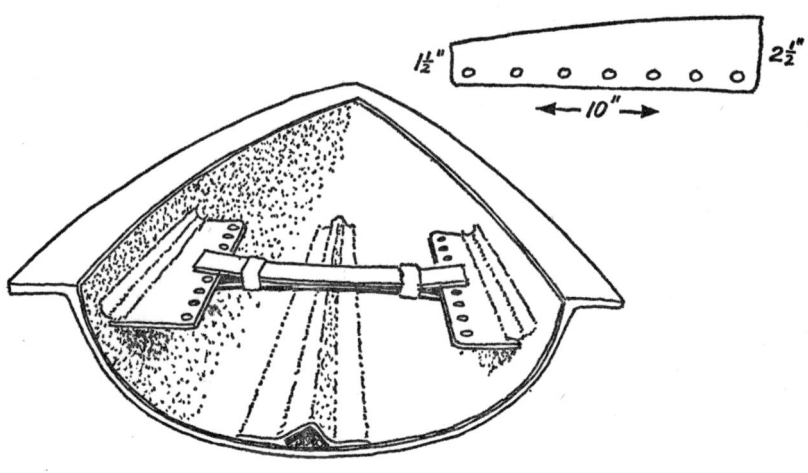

Fig. 47

Make a jig to hold the flanges in position. You should place them so that your feet, or the user's feet, will come about half way along the flange when in place. Tall people should arrange the footrest so that its furthest end will accommodate their feet, short people should arrange it with the footrest just at the nearer end. The jig can be made of two thin slips of hard-

board and some electrician's tape. The hardboard slips should
be longer than the gap between the flanges, and about 2–3 in.
wide. Tape them together about 3 in. from each end. Jam the
flanges into the gap between the slips. Thus held, parallel and
level, they can be laid into place, with the rough side of the
laminate upwards, thus giving the joint to the hull a stronger
hold. Cut six narrow strips of glass mat, not quite as long as
each flange, and about 1 in. wide. Mix a very small quantity
of resin, and laminate them into position, three strips to each
side. Form well down with the brush, ensuring that there are
no rough edges to snag feet or kit when in use. The footrest
bar can be made later. It is not essential to join the flanges to
the hull on the underside, but if you do, ensure that the smooth
underside is roughened before positioning. It does make a
stronger job.

By now the resin used in the hull will be beginning to set,
or gel. To check this, just flick the waste edge that sticks up all
around the mould with the finger. If it is soft and wet, it is
not yet ready for trimming. If it is springy, slightly rigid, then
it is right for trimming. If it is hard, and very rigid, then it is
too late for an easy trim, and you will have trouble. But it isn't
difficult to catch it at just the right moment, if you are expect-
ing it. Take a sharp knife, and trim right round, quickly.
(See Fig. 48) Trimming the deck will probably have to wait
until another half an hour to an hour has passed.

Now laminate the cockpit. Put the pieces of glass ready.
Mix up just under 2 lb. of laminating resin, and use a 2-in.
brush. If you are making a white cockpit, and you use a brush

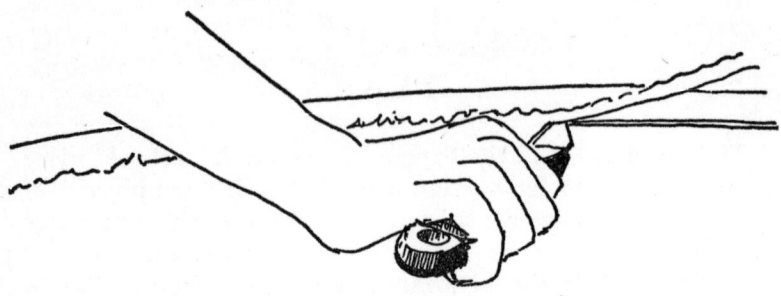

Fig. 48

that has still got some colour in it, you will have smears of colour showing in the laminate, and this shines through the gel-coat and spoils the job. With black it doesn't matter so much, but it is good to cultivate habits of clean workmanship.

Try to stand the cockpit at a convenient height so that you can walk all around it easily. Cover the job with wet resin, and lay on the first piece right across the seat, ensure that is centrally placed. Paint resin liberally all over this sheet, but don't try to work it at all. Take short pieces of glass strip and put them around the rim. Butt joint them, but do ensure that joints in different layers do not coincide. Again simply slop on the resin, and do not work it. This whole first layer can take as little as three minutes to make. Five minutes is more usual. Now form the glass down on to the mould, all over. Immediately start to lay up the second layer, and keep going until all four layers are in place. Now roll down with the hard roller. Take the last of the resin, and brush firmly all over, slightly fluffing up the surface, then firming it down. Leave to harden until ready for trimming.

You can leave the job at this stage if you wish, but take care that the deck is trimmed clean, and the cockpit will be ready for trimming in about an hour. If the workshop is handy to home, just remember that the job is setting off, and you can go in for a while.

Joining up
Let us assume that it is the next day. The deck and hull and cockpit have been trimmed. The footrest flange jig has been removed. The deck is laid in place over the hull, and then joined together with nuts and bolts about every foot or so. The holes in the mould flange will ensure alignment of the two parts, although old moulds tend to have worn out holes, and so the register is lost. Arrange two strong cords from beams in the roof, or if you cannot do that, chock the moulds up on edge on a high bench, as nearly as possible with the centre of the cockpit hole at shoulder height. The best way to arrange the cords is to tie a bowline loop at one end of the cord, sling it up over a beam, and then bring the other end back through the loop, and secure it with a thumb knot. The cords should be

about half the length of the canoe apart, too far apart and the canoe will slip out between the slings. To raise the canoe, put your shoulder under it and lift it to the height required whilst tying the knot to the loop.

The glass strips are cut. These should be about $2\frac{1}{2}$ in. wide and 3 ft. long. The 14 ft. canoe will require 10 of these joining strips. Make the pole ready by squaring off one end with pliers, so that the shaft of the 2-in. brush just fits. If it is a tent pole still in service, it need not be deformed, and the brush handle can be shaved instead. The spike at the other end of the pole is necessary, but if there isn't one, then jam a piece of wood into the end of the pole and whittle it down to a pencil end, a short smooth spike is what is required.

Mix up about $\frac{3}{4}$-lb. of coloured gelcoat, and stir thoroughly. Dose the inside of the joint with this resin, about 2 in. each side of the joint crack. The idea is to fill the crack with gelcoat resin, which forms a seal to stop the laminating resin dripping through afterwards. The resin is applied by using the brush on the end of the pole. As soon as one side is done, which takes less than five minutes, turn the whole thing over in the slings, and work from the other side; or in the case of a set of moulds propped

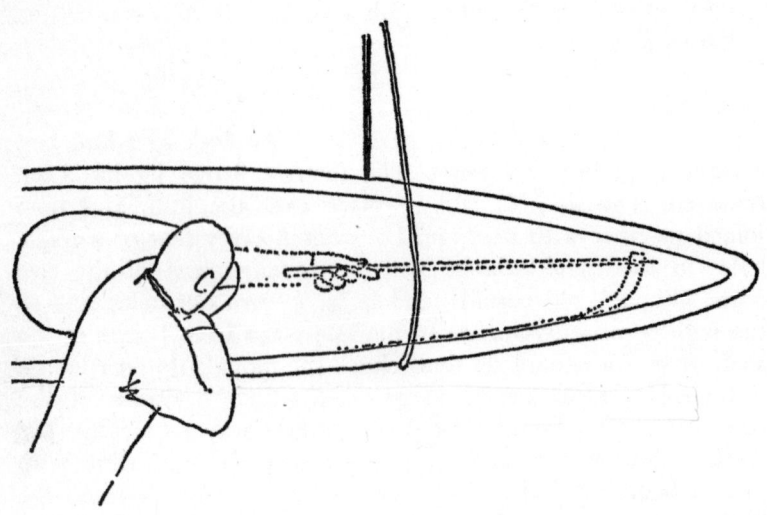

Fig. 49

up on a bench, turn the whole thing end for end, and then over, so as to get at the other side. Again, paint in a good layer of gelcoat over the joint.

Immediately, mix some laminating resin in with the gelcoat which has already been mixed, total required about $\frac{3}{4}$-lb., and add the necessary amount of catalyst for the extra resin. No need to add colour. Stir thoroughly, and set aside. It will start to set quite soon, as a large part of it is already half way towards gelling. Poke the spike end of the pole through one end of a piece of dry glass. Poke it right up to the end of the canoe, and use your other hand to pull the free end into line. Twiddle the pole between your fingers and ease it back. The end of the glass strip should slip off the pole and lie in place. Use the pole to stroke the strip down on to the joint. Carry on doing this first one end, then the other, then the next strip. After two strips at each end you can lay the pole aside and put the last strip in by hand. The strips should just butt up against one another. All this will take less than five minutes. Now start painting resin on to the glass, evenly starting at the far end and working towards the cockpit area. As soon as the joint strip has been thoroughly covered with resin, use the brush to smooth down the wetted glass, using it first on edge in a fishtailing way, then flat to smooth it down. This again should take less than five minutes, or at the most not more than seven. By now the resin may be turning a little stringy, so be quick. Turn the mould over again, and put the glass in to the other side as described. If you made a good job of it, the first side will stay happily in place. If you made a bad job of it, with not enough or too much resin on it, dry patches, and not sufficient smoothing down, it will drop off, and you will be festooned in soggy strips of wet glass, and you will be cursing the job and the mess. It usually gives you a slight warning, a sort of gentle sighing noise as air slips behind the resin-wet strips just before it drops. Do not try to rescue it, write it down against experience, and at once rake it out and throw it away, and start again later.

There is a risk of this happening, but not a very serious one. You may wish to play safe first time, and simply do one side at a time, waiting for several hours between sides. But I always do the job now, as described above. It is quick, neat, economical and effective. At this point mix up about a $\frac{1}{4}$-lb. of resin and glass scraps, and separate this into two blobs. Ram one blob into each end of the canoe, this is the end block.

Clean the tools, remembering to clean the pole thoroughly. Set the moulds level, it doesn't really matter which way up they are, and leave for several hours. If you want to get the cast out in a hurry, set the moulds upside down, put a fan heater on end on blocks or boxes under the cockpit, set to blow hot air into the cockpit. It could then be ready in less than an hour. If you do open up a set of moulds, and all the joint has not set, then immediately put the cast back into the moulds, and bolt up again.

While the joint is hardening, it is possible to take the cockpit off the mould, and to clean it up and make it ready for fitting to the canoe. If the mould is in good condition, and if the trimming of the cockpit has been neatly done at the right time, it will come off easily. However, when the waste edge has not been properly trimmed, it tends to lock on to the mould edge, and so stop the cast coming off. A typical way in which the cast keys on to the mould is at the front edge of the seat if the cast waste-edge bulges inwards. The cast then cannot rise up-

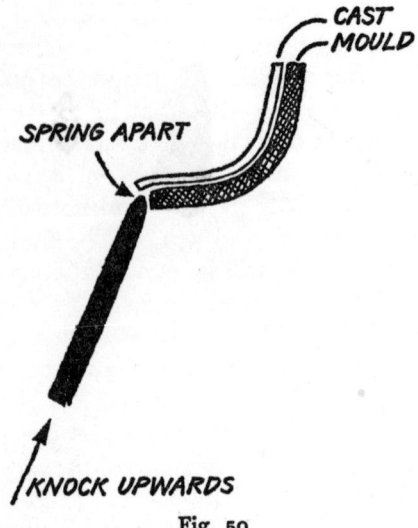

Fig. 50

wards to come off the mould, and so is locked on until you saw the waste edge off. Then, the novice will find that he cannot keep a straight line with the coping saw, and so the errant blade will carve out pieces from the edge of the mould; and one loses one's deposit on hire of the moulds.

Assuming a clean cast, then take the bolster, and, holding the mould and seat firmly down on to the top of the bench, look for a slight projection at the edge of the cast, and knock it up with the bolster held at right angles to the joint line. DO NOT try to enter the bolster blade directly between the cast and the mould. If you do you will surely damage the surface of the mould. It should spring off first time. Work from the front of the rim to the side, and from the back of the rim to the side. Then, after a gap has been made, insert the bolster blade between the cast and the mould and start to lever gently upwards. If the seat part seems stuck, take the mould off the bench, and hold it at knee height above a hard floor which is clean and flat. Drop the seat mould on to one part of the curve of the seat and then on to the other. The blow is on the seat, and from that height should cause no damage. Higher than that and you will almost certainly fracture the seat and probably the mould as well. The seat should then pop up off the mould. Old moulds, or copy moulds taken from old designs, tend to bulge outwards in the middle of the seat side, and this gives the mould a sort of bottle shape, over which the seat must be sprung to get it off the mould. This is a fault of 'old age' in moulds.

Having taken the cast off the mould, lay the cast aside, and clean up the mould. Now brace the seat cast between the bench edge and the hip. Use the file in the two hands, and cut the rim clean, so as to dispose of the slight edge. The mould edge will leave its mark on the cast. I use an electric drill with a coarse cutting disc in it at this stage, in order to trim it quickly. Commercial firms use pneumatic tools turning at 20,000 rpm with 2-in. diamond tipped wheels. Filing is the slowest way.

Nevertheless, brace up, and hold the seat firm, and start filing. You will soon appreciate the reason for getting a good trim off the knife first shot. If the edge to be trimmed off is wider than an eighth of an inch, then cut it with the coping

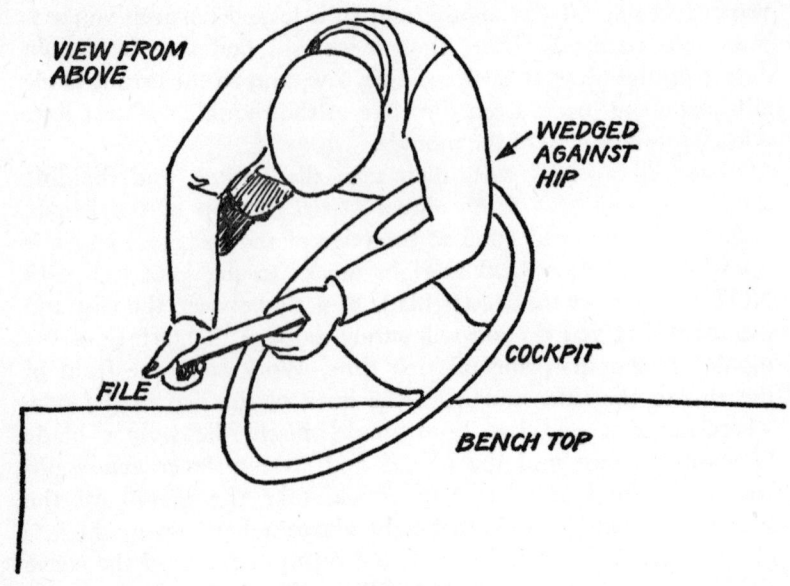

Fig. 51

saw first. Get the outer edge of the rim really clean, and rounded. If you don't, and leave a sharp edge, it will (a) cut your fingers, or someone else's, and (b) cut your spray deck to ribbons after a while, letting the wet in.

If you can get someone to stand patiently while you file the edges, and hold the job firm then that is much easier. Now file the inner edges of the rim, and the edges of the seat. Some seat moulds are wider at the sides than they need to be. In that case you may have to saw off some of the side. As you sit in a canoe, your thighs lie to each side, and the muscle is relaxed, and so lies against the edge of the seat and presses under the inner edge of the rim. Do, please do be sure that these edges are smooth and clean. You could be in that cockpit for five hours at a time, if you go in for advanced sea trips. Any faults in seat finishing will surely show by then.

Having finished the cockpit off very neatly with coarse, and then fine rubbing paper, it is ready for joining into the canoe. Whilst you are still waiting for the joint to become hard, make the footrest bar.

Footrest

Be warned. If you do this badly, or use the wrong method, you could be setting up a trap which could kill the paddler. The typical incident is that the canoe and canoeist rushes down upon an obstruction, and is unable to avoid it. Either there is a great rock, or tree root, or the sea bottom in a pearldive in surf. The feet are braced against the fixed footrest bar, which is bolted to the flange at each end. The canoe, and the footrest flanges stop with a mighty thud. The body and the feet slide straight on, bending a strong bar, ripping the flanges and the feet are in front of the bar, the heels hooked over the bar, or the toes under. Because of the damage and bend, its like a latch, and the more you pull back, the tighter is the bar jammed against the feet. The ends of the bar cannot move, so there you are, all worries about rent, rates of pay, loved ones, and so on about to end. You have between 20 and 30 seconds left to ponder these things during which you panic. At the end of this time you take in water, relax unworried, and quietly fade away, 2 minutes later you are a statistic.

The footrest system which is designed to avoid this trouble is the failsafe footrest. It is hinged at one end by a bolt, and simply rests against a stop at the other. You can press as hard as you like, and it remains solid. Maybe your feet get jammed over it. Pull back, and there is nothing to stop the bar releasing on one side, and so back it comes. You can buy these bars and brackets ready made up from Valley Canoe Products, who designed the system. However, you can make your own as follows.

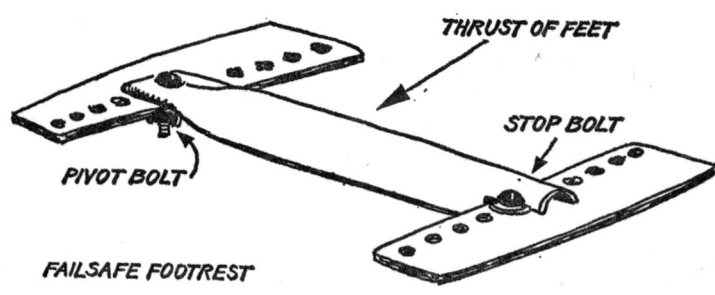

Fig. 52

Measure the distance between the inner edges of the footrest flanges. Add 2 in. to this, and cut that length of alloy tube. Flatten one end of the tube, file to a clean profile, and drill a hole about ¾-in. from the end of the flattened bit. Set the bar upright in a vice. File marks across the top edge of the tube, parallel, across the diameter, the distance between the lines being the thickness of the flanges plus a sixteenth of an inch for clearance. This slot must be dead parallel with the flattened end at the other end of the tube. File all edges clean. The drawing shows how the method works.

By now, the hull-deck joint should be about hard enough. 5 or 6 hours should ensure that in all but the coldest sheds. Put the moulds on a bench, deck uppermost. Take the bolster and drive it between the two flanges of the moulds at one end. Use the hammer to drive it in, but carefully, no great thumping whacks, or you will shatter the flanges. Having got it in, brace your two hands on to it, and your hands and wrists against your hip and thigh, and then press forward with the strength of your legs, levering up and down slightly as you slide the wedge along the gap between the flanges. You may have to have someone holding the moulds steady as you push around. Quite quickly the air will be seen to be slipping between mould and cast, and you can lever away to get the air completely through the gap. Next, the cockpit hole edge must be eased out. Again, you MUST NOT drive a wedge directly between cast and mould. Find a slight projection on the trimmed edge of the cast, I often leave slight projections when trimming, and brace the bolster against this. Tap gently with the hammer at right angles to the rim edge, so as to spring the cast edge inwards. It will spring out straight away, but this is to break away the gelcoat link from cast to mould edge. Having gone all round, then lift again, at both ends at the same time, and bounce it gently up and down. If you have a mould which is very flat across the cockpit area, and is not braced, then do take care that you don't fold the mould. All being well, it should spring off. Lay the mould aside out of the way.

Put the canoe, still in the hull mould, on to the floor. Stand with one foot in the cockpit and the other foot on the hull mould flange. You may need a support. Brace your weight

Fig. 53

firmly down on to the flange. If it doesn't separate, then stamp on it, but lightly please.

Having started off one edge, then shift your weight from one flange to the other, and bounce the other edge loose. Now stand astride the moulds, hand down on to the flanges, have a helper to hold the mould steady at the other end, and brace your weight down on to the flange, easing the separation along the edge a little at a time. Do this fore and aft and make sure both sides are free. The ends may be locked in, so lay a piece of wood across the very end of the mould flange, and give the piece of wood a smart tap with the hammer. This should cause the cast to ease up in the mould. You can see by looking at the casting flash, and it should be about the thickness of a piece of paper up from the flange. Do that at both ends. Take hold of the cockpit rim at front and back, reverse your grasp, thumbs towards you, and with your helper holding the mould down, brace upwards firmly and so pop the cast out. If it doesn't come free, turn the job over and see if there is still evidence of the cast sticking to the mould underneath. If there is, thump it

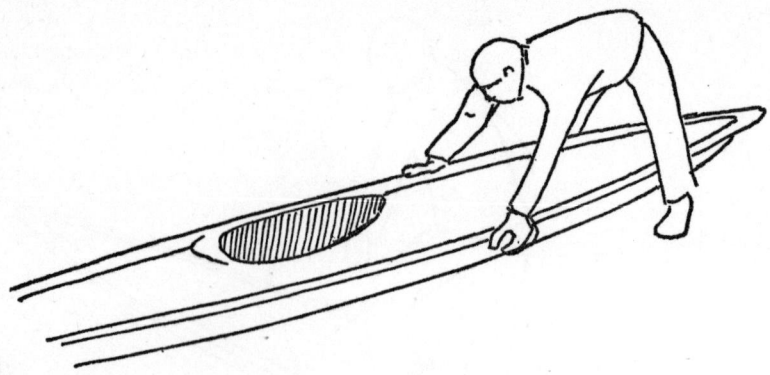

Fig. 54

with your fist, using the soft edge of your hand by the little finger. Do not clout it with your knuckles or you will surely bleed. If that doesn't work, you may have a 'sticker', and that is sad work. Next step is to take a pad of wood, lay it over the place where the adhesion is, and tap it with the hammer. If that doesn't shift it, hit it harder. If that doesn't work, send for an expert. Last of all you could try to slide slips of plywood between cast and mould, around the sticking patch. The plywood should be about 4 mm., about 2 ft. long and 3 in. wide, with rounded edges. By this time, if there is adhesion, you will see a characteristic milky bloom around the sticking patch, shot through with radiant flexion cracks. That of course means real trouble, and it happens about once in every two years for me one way or another. I always curse in just the same way.

Incidentally, if eventually you do separate the two parts, you can rescue the mould, as very likely it will be the cast that has stuck to the mould, and separation is achieved by ripping part of the surface of the cast away.

That is digressing, but I want to remind you of the need for proper preparation.

Most probably you will slide the canoe gently out of the mould, and it should glint in the light, and glitter beautifully. Lay it aside with care, and attend to the moulds. Take the side edge of the chisel, and run it along the flanges, laid across the width of the flange, and thus scrape off the hard resin that has bled through from the joint. Dust the mould out with a rag, and bolt both deck and hull together with four bolts, one at each end and one at each side, to hold it together and to stop rubbish dropping into it. Put it out of the way, ready for the next canoe.

Put the canoe on the bench and admire it. I always do, and its many a canoe I've had the pleasure to admire. Go all round it and break off the casting flash, use the side edge of the chisel, or the side of the bolster, and chip away with chipping strokes. This is to reduce the possibility of cutting oneself on the sharp edges. It must be trimmed in any case, so do it as soon as possible. At the same time, trim the cockpit hole edge, so that the cockpit drops in neatly. Some moulds are made so that the hole edge is higher and narrower than it need be; in this case you must cut back the edge of the hole, possibly half an inch. Use a coping saw after marking the line to cut with a felt pen.

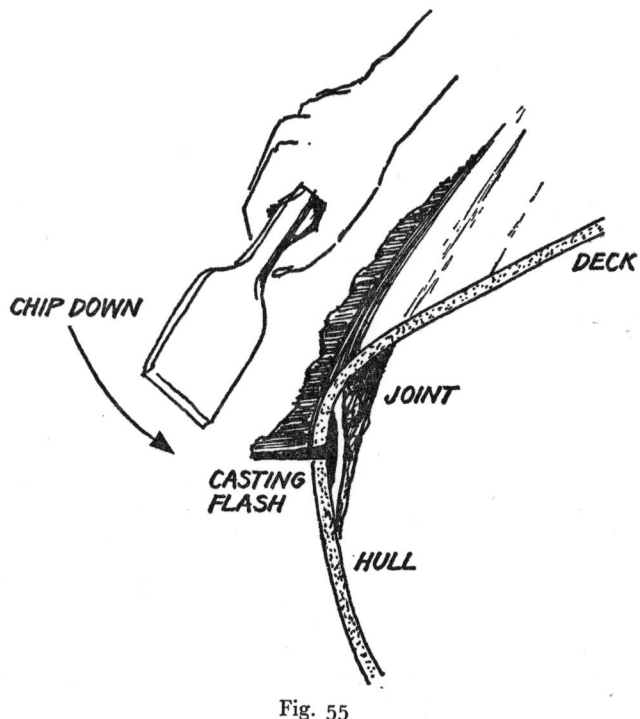

Fig. 55

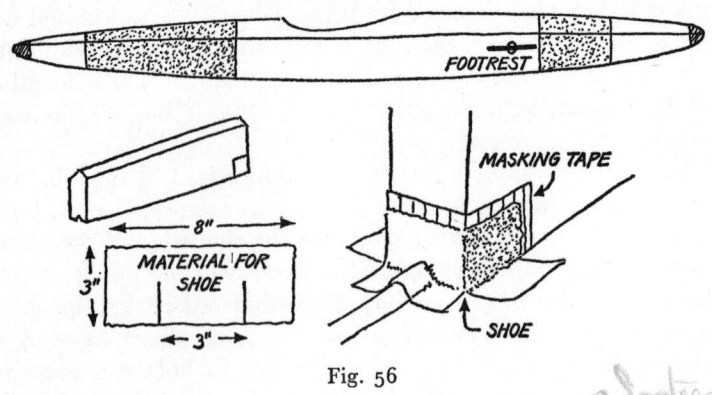

Fig. 56

Before the cockpit is fitted, the buoyancy block must go in. You may fit as much as you can, or you may wish to leave some space for equipment. It may be that you will wish occasionally to rely upon the buoyancy of equipment in watertight bags, such as a sleeping bag. This makes excellent buoyancy. In that case you should order air bag buoyancy and not fit fixed buoyancy blocks. However, if you wish to go for rough water canoeing, the decks will be supported by blocks of polystyrene foam. In that case you should fit them at this stage as follows.

Measuring the blocks to fit is not easy. Sometimes patterns for these will be supplied, and all you do is to draw around these and cut out the foam using a cross cut saw, or even a hacksaw blade, one end wrapped in a cloth. First the profile must be cut, then the cross section. Stand the canoe on a table. Stand the block beside it where you want it to go. Take a felt pen and crouch down so that you see the profile of the canoe with the block behind it. Look as far back into the distance as you can, and pick some point. It may be the inside of the workshop wall, only six feet away. Aim as levelly as you can along your line of sight from a point on the deck ridge past one end of the block, to a mark on the wall. Put a mark from the pen on the block, on this line. Do the same at the other end, and between these two points draw a line which is parallel to the deck profile of the canoe. Go to the wall, and identify the mark you were working on. Estimate the depth of the canoe at the front end of the block, and measure downwards on the wall, and make another mark at that distance. Go back to the canoe, and now sight along underneath it, again drawing a line as required, using the lower mark on the wall to aim on. Now cut the profile of the canoe on to the block.

Now look at the deck camber of the canoe, at the front and at the back of the block. Estimate this, and draw a cross section both on the front and back of the block. Cut the camber of the deck, and hull bottom along the block. File to bring it to a smoother outline. If you have a hull stiffener in the canoe, then a longitudinal slot must be cut along the bottom of the block. Now it is tried for size. Do not drive it in tightly, as if you do it may not be possible to get it out. If it does jam, you can try having a helper squeeze the canoe where the block is jammed. Try and collapse the gunwales towards one another. This will cause the deck and hull to move apart slightly, perhaps allowing enough clearance to get the block out again. Do any more fitting that is required. Now protect the front lower end of the rear block, and the aft lower end of the front block with masking tape. This is to stop resin getting on to the polystyrene, as it melts it away very easily.

Now, being satisfied that the front and back blocks are properly placed, the end of the rear block nearest to the cockpit opening should be about 12 in. back from the cockpit rim; this allows day kit to be packed in. The end of the front block nearest to the cockpit should be just in front of the front of the footrest flanges. Cut two pieces of glass mat, each about 8 in. long by 3 in. wide. Two slits are cut, the distance between them being the thickness of the block. These are equally spaced on one side of the glass, and extend half way through the width of the piece. Pre-wet with a little catalysed gelcoat, and place over the end of the block where the masking tape has been put. Smooth into place with the brush. It will probably be necessary to use the extension pole when fixing the front block. If you make a mess of it, pull the piece out, and start again. Do not try to persevere with a spoiled piece it is only a waste of time. Leave to set.

Now to fit the seat to the deck. Try the cockpit in place, and make sure it is a good fit. A slightly wobbly edge to the cockpit

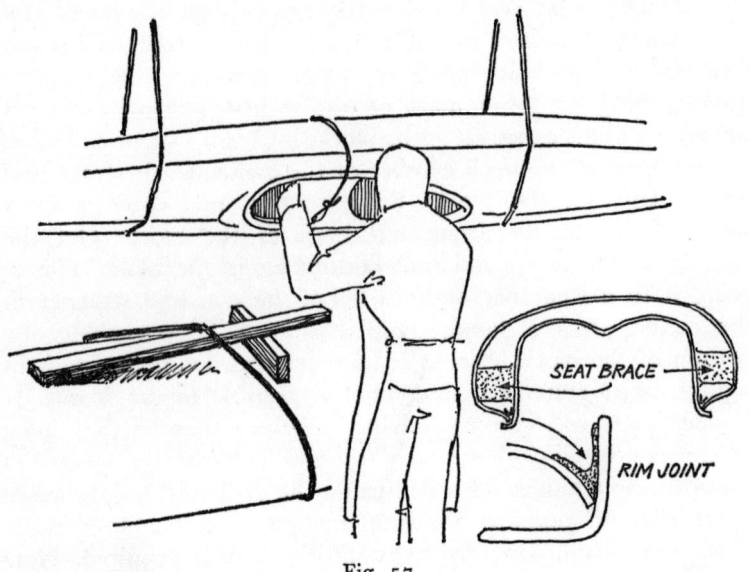

Fig. 57

hole is tolerable, but avoid it if you can. Get a length of cord, and make a bowline at one end, about 3 in. across will do. The cord goes right round the cockpit and holds it into the deck. Take the loose end of the cord back through the loop at one end, and tighten up by pulling the free end tight whilst pushing in the opposite direction on the same tail of cord but on the opposite side of the loop.

Some, in fact many, cockpit rims do not fit the deck hole accurately. The cord that holds the cockpit in place can be tightened up by wedging it between the bottom of the canoe and the cord. A piece of wood about 2 ft. long is pushed under the cord lengthways, and another piece of wood is slipped under the first and pushed towards where it is crossed by the cord, thus tightening up the cord. The front and rear ends of the rim may tend to spring upwards. This can be held by small clamps, or if you do not have these, drill small holes at the front and back in the part of the rim on the inside. Jam matchsticks, or fine screws into these holes so as to keep the rim in place. They should come out later.

Now sling the canoe upside down about shoulder height, so

that one can just stand up with the head inside the cockpit. Tilt the cockpit hole towards one side, so that you can work to one side. Put ready two strips of glass mat $1\frac{1}{2}$ in. by 3 ft., a screwdriver, a 2-in. brush, and a piece of cardboard about 2 ft. by 1 ft. This is the wetting-out board. Mix up about a quarter pound of gelcoat, and 3 ml. of catalyst, and you can begin.

Tear off a piece of mat, just long enough to fit behind the seat flange. It is better to do the most difficult piece first. Paint gelcoat all round the inside of the cockpit rim that you can see, and wet the inside of the deck for about 2 in. Paint resin all over the piece of mat, and immediately, before the binder softens, drape the strip into place behind the seat flange, or seat side might better describe it. Do not press it down into the wedge-shaped gap, but leave it to soften first. Now place strips of glass, pre-wetted with gelcoat resin, all along the inside of the rim from centre front to centre back on one side. The strips should just meet at the ends, no need to overlap.

When one side is done, tilt the canoe the other way, step to the other side, and do it. If you are working where you cannot sling the canoe, then prop it between two chair backs, and work sitting down. You will need to weight the chairs so that they do not fall over. Having put wet strips on each side, go back to the first side, and using the screwdriver blade, or better still a thin-bladed palette knife, push the strip down into the gap, starting behind the seat side and working along. Follow with the brush and make sure the glass and resin are smoothed down, as prickly lumps here over the knees will cause havoc later when the canoe is in use. After the resin has hardened off a little, the waste edge standing up along the inside of the rim can be trimmed off.

The seat, if simply fixed in at the rim, can sway about like a stiff hammock. When one is engaged in sudden changes of balance, as on a rapid river, or surf, or on short choppy waves with the sea aft, then the slight shifting of the seat is most unsettling and to be avoided. The way to do that is to fit seat braces between the seat side and the inside of the hull. Some fit a single brace centrally right under the seat, which is great while it lasts, but it generally lasts about two trips, as the slightest bump underneath causes it to break away. The braces should go in fairly high up the side of the canoe, as any stiffening on the turn of the hull to the bottom may cause localised stress cracking.

With the wetting-out board ready as before, and a 2-in. brush cleaned and ready for use, cut two pieces of glass mat, each about 3 in. by 9 in., for each side of the canoe. That's four pieces in all. Mix up about ¼-lb. of gelcoat. Laminating resin is so much wetter that the brace will probably become too soggy and fall sideways out of place. With the canoe still in the slings, lay one piece of glass on the wetting-out board, wet it with resin, place another piece on top of that and wet that too. Do not work it through.

Immediately the resin is on the glass, pick it up in the fingers, and place it between the outside of the seat side, and the inside of the hull. Smear the ends of the strip so that they lay flat, one end against the hull and the other end against the seat side. Use the brush to smooth it into place. Check it and prop it in place with the brush until it is just balanced in place. Do the same for the other side. Turn the canoe dead level and upside down, check the braces have not slipped, then leave it until the resin has set. The slightest bump can upset the braces and cause them to slip.

When this has set, you can take the canoe down from the slings, and file off any rough edges around the cockpit and seat. Remember that your whole body weight is going to be slung in this seat for possibly hours on end, it may be bounced up and down very vigorously from time to time, and it will probably turn over occasionally. So the whole thing must be comfortable for the body within, no rough or sharp edges. One way to improve the comfort of the seat and rim, is to smear filler into the gap between rim edge and deck inside, so as to fill the gap. This can either be a commercial filler, or your own mix, made from calcium carbonate powder and resin, as a stiff paste. This goes in on top of the glass strip already placed. To improve the comfort for the knees, cut two pieces of neoprene rubber, if you have some wet suit material about, and stick this in place over where the knees go, using rubber glue. The commercial people use polyethylene foam pads about half an inch thick.

Now drill two holes in the canoe, one at each end. The idea

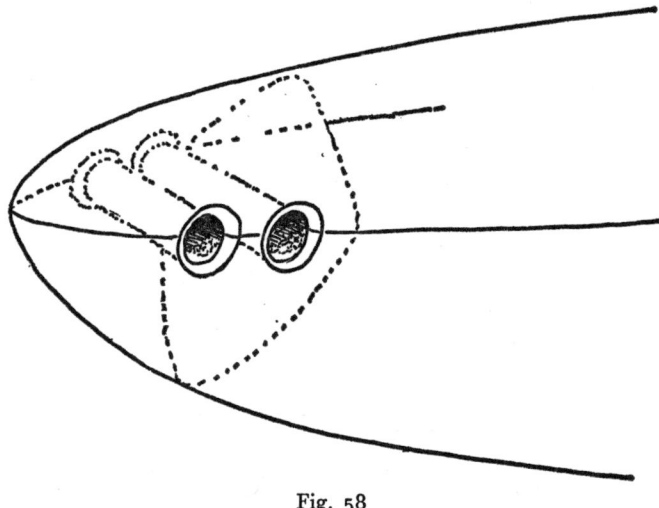

Fig. 58

is to go through the end block, so that leaks into the hull are
not introduced.

Rigging the canoe
Two holes are drilled in each end, about $\frac{5}{16}$-in. diameter, right
through the ends from side to side, usually on the joint line, and
if you have it right, through the end block. If you strike open
space, which you can feel as the drill slips through, then look
inside at the end and see if you have broken through. If you
have, mix up a little more resin and glass mat, and stuff this up
inside the end, and later re-drill the hole.

Now the trim stripe is put on. Lay the tape along the hull,
about a quarter of an inch above the joint line, and another
strip of tape about a quarter of an inch below the joint line.
These must be parallel and without kinks. The narrower the
line is, the better it looks, although a big fat wide band can
look quite well if it is bold enough and straight enough, and it
can hide a multitude of sins, such as rough edges from old
moulds, or wide joint gaps from poor moulds or bad building
techniques, or long bubbles under the gelcoat which break
through, and are unsightly. (The way in which to lay tape
along a joint line is described in mould building, attaching the

E

temporary flange.) I find that it is useful to widen the gap at the ends in a curving way, so as to include the holes at the ends.

Mix up about $\frac{1}{4}$-lb. of gelcoat, with colour which matches the cockpit for aesthetic satisfaction, and go round the whole job quickly, simply brushing resin on, and not bothering too much if it goes over the edge of the tape, although try to keep it within bounds. Bubbles will appear, and open, and the gaps will show down into the depths of the joint gap. Go round again, and using the brush in a sideways motion, smear resin into the gap and try to fill it up. Do not spend a lot of time on this, but go right round doing what you can. Now go round again, work on the few remaining gaps, and fill them. Now go right round gently stroking the resin with the brush so as to leave a smooth cover of resin without pips or lumps on it. You must be quick about this, as the resin may begin to set within ten minutes, especially in warm conditions.

As soon as you have finished with the brush, pull off the tape, and leave it to harden. After it has hardened, you may need to re-drill the end holes. If you drill the holes after putting on the trim stripe, you may crack the stripe round the hole, which can be unsightly. Now fit a $\frac{5}{16}$-in. drill bit into the drill, and drill four pairs of holes near to the cockpit. (This is only if you wish to fit a deck line.) The holes should be about an inch apart. Each pair should be just on the edge of the deck about 2 in. from the joint line, and in line with either the front or the rear of the cockpit hole. In front of the cockpit, about 15 in. forward, drill one hole on one side of the deck and one hole on the other side of the deck, again about 2 in. from the joint line. This pair of holes is for the elastic paddle-park.

Decide what diameter the end loop should be. This loop is fitted through the end hole nearest to the cockpit. Cut a piece of cord about 6 in. longer than that, to allow for the knot, or if it is to be made as a grommet, its length must be three times the circumference of the loop required. Each of the loops to be fitted to the deck near to the cockpit must be cut ready, either as a knotted loop or as a grommet. See Fig. 59. Having made the knots, or loops, then the holes must be sealed. Sling the canoe upside down, and make a patch about 2 in. in diameter, and stick it inside over knot and holes with gelcoat.

The end loops are already sealed off by the end blocks. The patches are left to harden before the deck line is strung through. The toggles are now fitted. Cut a piece of cord about a foot long. Push it through one hole in the toggle, and bring the end of the cord out through the end of the toggle. Tie a thumb knot, and then push the knot and cord back inside the toggle. Now push the free end of the cord through the end hole, and then through the second hole in the toggle, bringing it out through the other end of the toggle. Tie a knot as closely to the toggle as possible. Push this knot back inside the toggle, and pull tight. It improves the toggle, if it is whipped with suitable twine between the canoe deck and the underneath of the toggle. This makes the toggle stand up instead of trailing in the water, which is a drag. Now cut off about 2 ft. of 5 mm diameter elastic, and slip it through one of the holes in the deck for the paddle park. Reach inside, and tie a knot, figure of eight would be best. Pull the elastic tightly and slip it through the other hole. Pull it and stretch it across the deck so as to allow as much as possible inside the canoe. Tie a stopper knot (figure of eight) in that. Release gently, and the paddle park elastic should be firm across the deck.

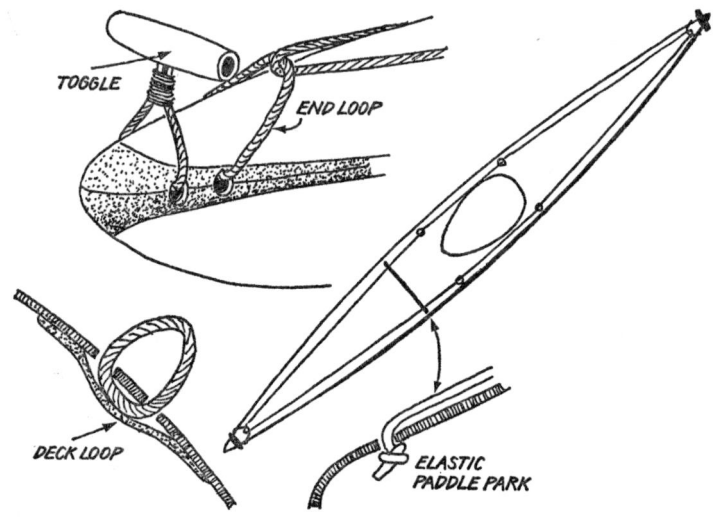

Fig. 59

Now that the deck loop patches are hard, the deck line can be fitted. It should be $\frac{1}{4}$ in. diameter laid cord, although braided will do. I prefer laid cord because I can splice it. The deck line should be about $2\frac{1}{2}$ times the length of the canoe. There are many ways of rigging a canoe, but the way which I find simplest and as effective as anything I've tried is as follows. It does not use expensive and heavy shackles, or jambing cleats, simple knots being quite sufficient. Start at the rear left deck loop, and splice a 3-in. long loop into one end of the deck line using this to anchor the deck line to the deck loop. I splice it on so that it cannot be removed. Having spliced it on, take it forward through the left fore side loop, then through the bow loop, then back through the two right side loops, through the stern loop, then forward through the loop to which it is anchored. Take the end across to the other side rear loop, and knot it there with a simple thumb knot.

Variations in Building Techniques

Colour variations

At the College where I now work, there is a member of staff who is a canoeist and a Welshman. His canoe is bright golden yellow all over, except for a rather beautiful representation of the Welsh Flag on the foredeck. This, if you didn't know, is a red dragon on a field which is green below and white above the half way mark. The detail on the dragon is black. There are five colours on this. When I have described how we did this then you will know how to tackle your own brightly coloured decoration.

The first requirement is that the mould shall be fully run-in, and that release agent, i.e. PVA fluid, is not required. The cast must separate from the wax polished surface. This is because we must use masking tape and 'Fablon' and this would peel off and remove any release agent.

Now it must be planned. The order in this case was as follows.

1. Paint in details in black
2. Red dragon filled in
3. White field put in
4. Green field put in
5. Yellow gelcoat for whole of canoe.

A sheet of 'Fablon' was obtained, large enough to allow the dragon to be drawn on the backing paper exactly as it is to appear on the finished job. If you draw on the shiny side, it comes out back to front. The details were impossible to put in as a stencil, so the whole outline was copied from a Welsh Flag, and the outline drawn in and cut out with a sharp knife. The backing paper was peeled off, and the dragon was stuck centrally on the foredeck. The inner edges of the 'Fablon' were carefully smoothed down firmly to the deck surface: any gap here and the gelcoat will creep along underneath.

Now, having an outline to work within, it was possible to mix up a tiny quantity of black gelcoat, and with a fine artist's brush, paint in the detail of the outline, heavier under the belly where it should be darker, a suggestion of scales, glaring eyes . . .

'Great big heed and great big gob and great big goggly eyes . . .' (Lambton Worm)

Pardon the diversion. A convincing outline was done free-hand. This is back to front of course.

This was left to harden for two hours, and then we came back, mixed up a little red gelcoat, and sloshed it merrily all over the black lines and the cut-out shape of the dragon. As soon as this was done properly, the 'Fablon' was at once stripped off, taking care not to let it drape back on to the red gelcoat and so smear it. This left an accurate shape of the red dragon, but the lines could not be seen, being buried under the red gelcoat. Remember you are looking at the inside of the outside of the canoe deck. If you wait until the gelcoat is hardening before stripping off the 'Fablon' you will peel off bits of the red and so leave a raggy inaccurate edge.

Again we went away for two hours, and then came back, and with great care tested the resin for hardness. We then surrounded the dragon with a rectangle of masking tape, and marked this off horizontally half way with a strip of tape of which the top edge was exactly on the half way mark. We tried not to stick it firmly to the red dragon, but of course it had to be firmly stuck down to the bare deck. The top half of the field was now coated in white gelcoat. The tape was removed at once, first the strip across the half way mark, and then the upper half of the 'frame', but this was cut off at the half way mark by pressing down on the tape with a knife blade and pulling the tape up against the edge. You must NEVER cut down on to the mould surface. This was left for another two hours.

Now we returned to cover the lower part of the field in green gelcoat which we mixed from some yellow and a bit of blue. We mixed the pigment first to the colour required, and then mixed that with the gelcoat resin. The remaining masking tape was pulled off, and another two hour wait ensued. Finally, about 6 pm, we mixed up the gelcoat for the deck and hull, golden yellow, and painted this all over everything. Everything that had to be covered, that is. It doesn't matter if you cover the back of the flag, because the face of it by now was showing a red dragon on a green and white field, with a yellow surround. The canoe was laid up with yellow resin, and the resulting job was really quite striking. You can speed up the gelcoat job by heating with a fan heater, the warm air being kept down on to the colour by laying a polythene sheet over it all, held up by cross supports of bits of wood, or in our case short lengths of alloy poles. One end of the sheet lies just over the front of the heater and the heater itself must be kept cool. Once it heats up an automatic cut-out operates and shuts it off, and you have no heat at all then. The danger here is, if the sheet droops down when it becomes warmer, it may touch and smear the gelcoat.

Simple colour jobs, such as a go-faster stripe, can be done with masking tape, again on a wax polished surface, as follows. Lay the tape just where you want the stripe. The stripe will be the same width as the tape. Lay the gelcoat for the deck all over the mould, including the surface of the tape. Peel off the tape. Allow to harden, then fill in the colour for the stripe.

Surf ski joining
The unusual advantage of the surf ski is that it is a completely closed boat, and the paddler sits slotted into the deck, but he has no access to the rest of the boat under the decks. These are completely sealed off. Give yourself pause for thought. How to do you join up a boat which is completely enclosed? There isn't any way in which to get at the joint inside . . . is there? The commercial builders so far have built rather horrible things with external flanged joints which any paddler will tell you is just not on. Looks a bit like a mobile mould. There must still be a joint at the widest point. So far I've solved it this way, but I do not claim originality for it, although I arrived at this conclusion quite independently. It is included here because it is my belief that a lot more boats will be built this way in future.

The deck and the hull joint is made in the usual way, but the cockpit area is a very large hole. The inside edges of this hole turn downwards into the cockpit hole, and the inturned

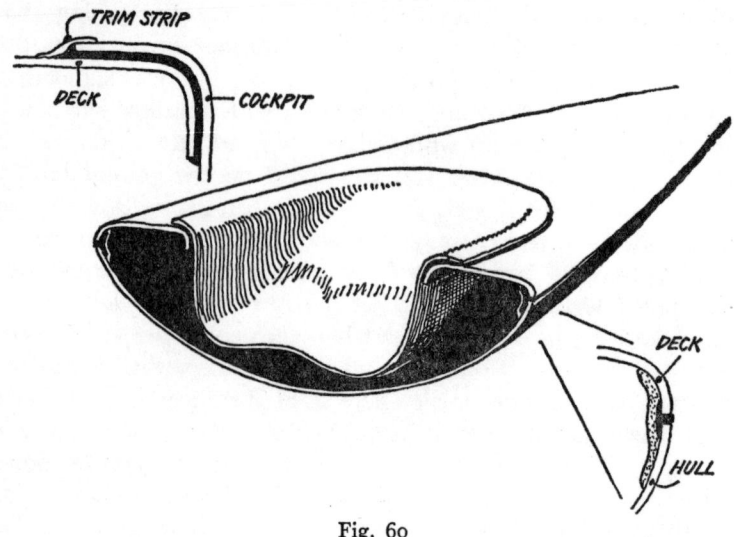

Fig. 60

flange is about 1½ in. wide. When the boat is made and removed from the mould, this surface is roughened. The cockpit is now made. Because it is not shot through with holes it can be made of three or even two laminations thus saving weight. No seat braces are required either, as the whole structure is self stiffened.

The still wet cockpit on its mould is placed on the ground, right way up of course. The hull-deck assembly is prepared by roughening, the rim to be joined is coated with gelcoat, and the assembly is placed upside down on to the cockpit assembly. Because this is still wet it can accept any slight irregularities in the parts. When set, it is turned the right way up and the mould is sprung out of the cockpit. The edge of the cockpit casting is prepared as for the joint stripe on the side of the finished boat, and a gelcoat seal is run around the cockpit-deck joint. Pop rivets could also be used, but these corrode.

A building method that hasn't been tried yet
Several methods of building canoes were tried and used commercially and successfully, but the advent of grp and easily available moulds rather cut the ground out from under them.

Well, one method that I lay awake dreaming about is as follows. It has never been tried, but I feel sure it has some use for someone somewhere. Its a method of building a stringer and canvas canoe inside a simple collapsible jig, and does away with the need for awkward plywood frames.

Obtain some hardboard sheets. Two sides are required, each as long as the canoe plus a foot at each end, each as deep as the canoe plus 4 in. Then cross frames are required, each as deep as the side frames, and each as wide as the widest frame shape plus 4 in., and as many cross frames as there are sections drawn on the plan. If the common interval is 12 in., then the side frames are marked off at these intervals. Small holes, say $\frac{1}{8}$-in. diameter are drilled in pairs each side of where the cross frame will abut on to the side frame. Matching single holes are drilled in the edge of the cross frames, so that the whole can be wired together like a great egg box. It can be collapsed flat, or dismantled for storage or transport. To stop it distorting in use, a base plate is wired on to the bottom at each end, it need be as wide as the widest space between the side frames, and about two feet long. This will hold it all rigid enough. The

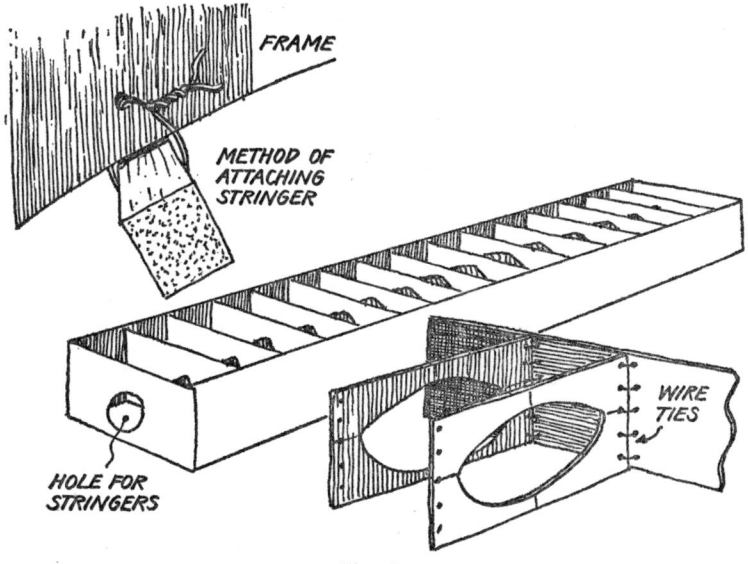

Fig. 61

structure will be a bit bendy. The addition of the stringers in due course will stiffen it all up.

Before the cross frames are all wired into place, the centre vertical line and the gunwale horizontal line for each section is marked on to each frame so that each will register exactly with each other; otherwise distortions will be built into the finished framework. Now the various section shapes are traced on to the cross frames, and they are cut out exactly.

Decide how many stringers there are to be, and where they are to appear on each section. Mark these stringer positions off on each frame, and drill a small, $\frac{1}{8}$-in. hole about an inch in from the section-shaped hole in each cross frame, just where the stringer is to go. Now assemble the whole jig, and set it dead level, using winding sticks to take out any wind. (*See page* 81 for method.)

Obtain as many stringers as you need, full length, and, say, $\frac{5}{8}$-in. x $\frac{3}{8}$-in. section. I would suggest nine or ten for the hull, and four or five for the deck. Lay all the stringers inside the jig, inserting them through the spaces between the end frames. Now lace them into position, tight up to the inside of the cross frames, wiring through the holes already drilled. Having set up the whole structure, and again checked for wind, take some

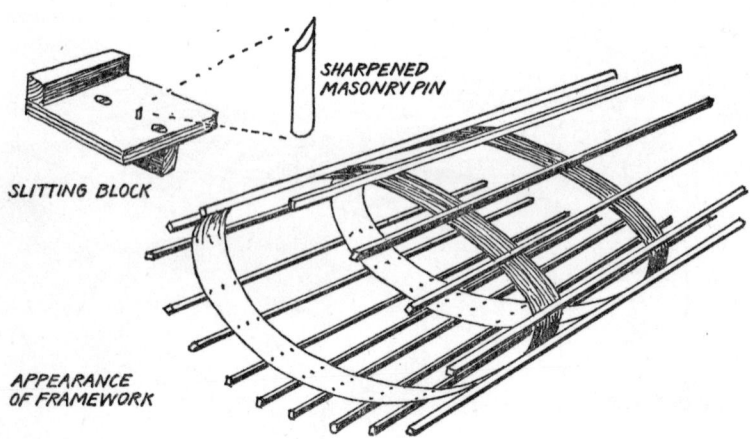

SHARPENED MASONRY PIN

SLITTING BLOCK

APPEARANCE OF FRAMEWORK

Fig. 62

thin ($1\frac{1}{2}$ mm) birch plywood, WBP at least (water and boil proof). Slice this into strips with a home-made stripper (See Fig. 62). Bend these around inside the stringers, and set them about 8 in. apart. Make up some suitable wood glue, waterproof, and glue the stringers and the bent frames where they cross each other. Bend into place, and staple through, using an industrial stapler, from the frame into the stringer. The staples can be left in, but they do corrode. Now decide where the cockpit is to go, and using some 4 mm marine plywood, cut side decks so as completely to surround the cockpit hole. They should extend 2 ft. forward of the front of the cockpit and about 6 in. aft, and run down to the gunwale stringers. These are then glued and screwed down on to the top surface of the stringers. The cockpit hole is then built up to make a rim to take a spray deck.

You will see that this method builds the hull and deck as one unit, and if you want to play about with the strip frames, you can wind them into two spirals of opposite 'thread', and so make a sort of geodetic structure like the Wellington bombers of the late thirties. The whole structure when finished is released from the ties to the frames, and the frame dismantled. It does just occur to me that to have the deck section of the jig so made as to lift up and release the canoe, without needing to strip down the whole jig would be an advantage. I think the method will produce very light and strong structures without the necessity for a great deal of carpentry skill. Bow and stern posts will be required in marine plywood to which the stringers must be chamfered and fixed, and that is about the most difficult part of it. Very few screws are required, but an industrial stapler and a box of staples will be required. The amount of very costly marine plywood is reduced, as waste from the cut-out parts of the usual sort of frames is eliminated.

I have thought of using this method for building plugs, and after building the structure I would stretch 9 oz. glass cloth all over it, and dose it with laminating resin, and leave this to harden. When firm, but still very flexible, the next stage would be to cover this with two laminations of glass mat, the rest being as detailed in the book. However, it is a method which produces a jig which can be used again and again, and this seems unnecessary for the one-off plug and so the method described in the book seems better for me to use. Who knows, perhaps in your part of the world this method, described but untried, may be just the thing for you. If you do use it, I'd be very pleased to hear how you get on with it.

How to export a canoe

You take it as hand luggage. With students and so on, who are generally hard up and travelling, this method has worked a number of times. Cast but do not join together a lightweight hull and deck and cockpit. The hull is 2-oz., and the deck 1-oz. laminate. The cockpit is 3-oz. laminate. Take a hacksaw and cut the deck and the hull across amidships. Tuck one end of the hull inside the other, and so too with the two halves of the deck. Bind together with masking tape, wrap in a sleeping bag, carry the cockpit in your hand or even cut the rim from the seat and stow both bits in your rucksack.

Somewhere in the depths of South America or Mexico or up some Norwegian fiord, unpack the bits, obtain some resin and glass locally, and stick the bits together. First the two halves of the hull are joined, taking care to line it up both directionally and for rocker. To do this drill $\frac{1}{8}$-in. holes in pairs each side of the cut at the top edge and wire this together with copper wire stripped from domestic electrical wiring, or use fine fencing or binding wire. Then join internally. You could even add another laminate if you like. Now join the fore part of the deck to the hull in a similar way. It is possible to locate one on the other simply with masking tape. Join this and it is easy as the whole structure is so light and easy to get at. Now, when that is hard, put the rear deck in place, and join together. Reassemble the cockpit, and add two more layers of glass and resin. Trim, file clean, and fix into canoe in usual way. You can even export a mould in a similar way. It is lightweight and not much good for production, but you can get a few boats out for your local club. I prefer to advise people to build a canoe rather than a mould.

Glossary of Terms

AFT Behind.

ARMATURE The rough central core of the plug.

BEAM Hull width

BILGE Usual in a ship. Space between inner hull and outer hull.

BOAT Almost anything, man-made, that is for moving on the water.

BROACHED Lying in the trough parallel to the wave crests. Dangerous. Precedes a roll-over.

BULKHEAD A vertical division between parts of a boat, usually watertight.

BUTT JOINT a joint made end to end.

BOTTOM DRAG A hull moving in water sets up bow and stern waves, both across the water surface and in depth. In shallow water these interfere with the bottom, and are reflected. The reflected waves then interfere with the incident waves. The bow rises, the stern squats, it slows down. The stern wave crests and overtakes the stern. To paddle is very difficult, it feels 'sticky'. The hull does not actually touch the bottom, but it feels as if the water had turned from water to treacle.

BOW The front end of the boat.

BUOYANCY Describes the floating qualities of a boat. If it floats it has positive buoyancy. If it sinks it has negative buoyancy. If it weighs 50 lb. but can, if pressed under the water, displace 500 lb., it is very buoyant. If it weighs 50 lb. and displaces 51 lb. it is not very buoyant. Also applied to material or bags put into a boat to assist it to float when waterlogged.

CALCULATION WATERLINE A line arbitrarily selected. The draught under this line may be 4 in. The displacement at this waterline can be calculated. It is usual to take three CWL, and to draw a displacement curve. Study of this curve will help one to 'prove' the design before committing materials and time to building the boat.

CAMBER The sideways slope, i.e. of a deck, or a road.

CANADIAN Usually prefacing the word 'Canoe' indicating country of origin of this archetype.

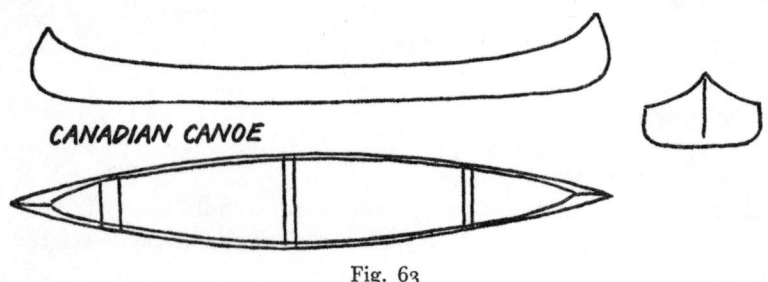

Fig. 63

CANOE Strictly speaking an open boat with decking only at the very ends.

CARBON FIBRE Strands of fibre made from carbon. Tensile strength is vastly more than that of an equal quantity of glass strands. Very expensive. In vogue for top class competition kayaks in late sixties.

CAST Sometimes called laminate. The object you have after laminating resin and glass inside a mould. Laminating a canoe is sometimes called casting a canoe.

CENTRE OF BUOYANCY Centre of gravity of the water which the canoe displaces.

CENTRE OF GRAVITY Centre of mass of the boat and its contents. The weight may be said to act through the centre of gravity, vertically downwards.

CENTRE OF LATERAL PRESSURE Suppose water flows at right angles to the side of the canoe or boat. It will exert a sideways pressure upon the boat. The sum total of all the pressure acting upon the hull may be said to act at the centre of lateral pressure. This notion is important when considering turning qualities.

CHINE When a canoe or kayak is made from sheets of material, such as plywood, then where they join is called a chine. Particularly applied to the edge where the bottom of the hull turns up into the side of the hull. Round-bottomed hulls do not have chines.

COCKPIT Where the paddler sits.

COCKPIT RIM The outer edge of the cockpit. The spray deck is attached to this.

COMMON INTERVAL The equal distance between each pair of adjacent sections on a drawing. The builder of the plug can then set out the frames at the proper distance along the spine.

CURING Setting resin is said to be curing.

CURVE Flexible; a strip of plastic with a core of flexible metal. Adjustable. French; sheets of rigid plastic with curved edges of varying radii. Fixed.

DATUM Either a point or a line, from which distances to other points are measured, either radially or at right angles.

DEADRISE In a chine boat, typically a speedboat, where the bottom rises up from the line of the keel to the chine. Usually referred to the slope at the transom. Could apply to a kayak with a chine construction.

DECK A lid on the hull to prevent water entering from above.

DECKLINE

1. *Rigging.* The cord which runs around the edge of the deck.
2. *Drawing.* The outline of the deck ridge in profile.

DIG As a spade digs into the ground, so does a skeg dig into the water. The plane of the skeg is in line with the line of travel of course. A certain amount of the quality of a skeg can be designed into the rear part of the hull, by making the rear part deeper without causing the keel line to take on any concave shape in profile. I call this giving the rear part of the hull extra dig.

DISPLACEMENT A canoe weighs 30 lb. Its paddler and equipment weigh 170 lb. It floats at rest on still water. It displaces 200 lb. of water.

DRAG When water flows over a surface, no matter how smooth that surface is, it tends to stick to it, a function of surface tension. The faster the boat goes, the greater is the drag. It applies primarily to displacement hulls. Sometimes called skin-drag.

DRAUGHT The depth of the lowest part of the hull, excluding keel or rudder, below the waterline.

DREADNOUGHT FILE A file with very coarse milled curved teeth.

FENCE In making a mould, it is necessary to put flanges on it. In order to do this, temporary fences are built at the widest point of the plug, i.e. along the line of greatest beam. The fence is removed after the first flange has been made.

FILLER Used by car body workers, and plug makers. Anything which will fill up a hole in a surface. Big depressions can be filled with a dough of gelcoat resin and glass scraps ($\frac{1}{4}$ in. deep or more). Small depressions are better filled with a commercial filler, usually a polyester resin with a powder mixed into it. A quick setting catalyst is added and the filler sets within ten minutes. I once used David's Isopon P38 a very good filler, but now I use a filler which is very similar to David's Isopon, which I obtain from Trylon, and which costs less.

FLANGE The edge of the mould, usually at right angles to the surface of the mould.

FLARE Usually applied to ships, especially clippers. The sides of the hull at the bow rise upwards and outwards from waterline to gunwale, in a hollow curve. This is called the flare. It has a practical purpose. The deeper the bow plunges into a head sea, the greater is the rate of increase in displacement at the bow per foot increase in depth immersed. Eskimo kayaks have a distinct flare at the bow.

FOOTREST No rest for canoeing feet. It really is a firm bar against which the canoeist can push with his feet, and so develop maximum power when required. It also helps him to jam his body tightly into the cockpit when in rough conditions. It must also fail-safe. (*See page* 119.)

FORE In front of.

FRAME A structural part of a canoe or plug, near enough the section at that point.

FREEBOARD Distance between waterline and gunwale line.

FREE SURFACE Imagine a tank empty. If it moves and stops it is done as a unit. Imagine that it is half full. If the tank is moving with its contents at rest within it, when it stops, the contents tend to continue moving. This makes stopping a difficult thing to do. A milk tanker driver I know always stops his articulated vehicle 5 feet short of a junction when it is half full, as after he stops the vehicle, the stopping load then humps it forward another 5 ft. Imagine the tank full. It is heavy, but there is no air in the tank, no place for the contents to surge forward. There is then no double effect when stopping. It's the same with canoes with some water in them. If the water is free to move about, if there is free surface, then there will be serious problems with all three types of stability.

GELCOAT A thick polyester resin. When set hard it makes the tough outer skin of a canoe. It is waterproof.

GELLING This is the condition of resin as it turns from liquid to solid.

GREEN Gelling resin, rubbery, no longer liquid but not yet hard, is said to be green.

GROMMET A loop or ring of stranded cord made by taking a piece of stranded cord slightly more than three times the circumference of the required ring. The strands are then separated, and each strand is then made into a ring by weaving the strand around and around itself. When it has been three times around, it looks like the original cord. Two tips. (a) there is a right way around and a wrong way around, trial and error will show you; (b) twist the strand each time it is turned around itself, in the opposite rotation.

GRP Glass Reinforced Plastic.

GUNWALE Corruption of gun wall. Applied to the line of maximum beam.

HARMONY As in music when some notes sound agreeable when played with others, some lines on a boat look right when seen in company with others. Some people are more sensitive to this than others, some see it, others do not. Practice assists one to appreciate this quality.

HERRING BONE A method of stiffening a thin laminate by cutting a narrow strip of glass mat, say 4 in. wide, and as long as required, wetting with resin, folding over lengthways, and sticking on to the laminate in a herring bone pattern. Typical on decks, not so much used now.

HULL That part of a boat which displaces water and which contains the crew and equipment.

ICF International Canoeing Federation. International governing body of the sport.

KAYAK Eskimo hunting boat. 'A floating butchers bench'. Hull completely decked apart from small central cockpit hole.

KEEL Lowest longitudinal timber of and on which a ship's hull is built. In a canoe it usually describes a position rather than a

F

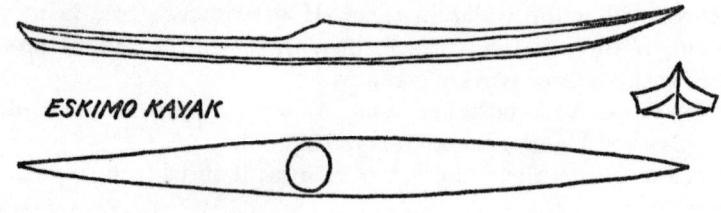

ESKIMO KAYAK

Fig. 64

structural piece. It means the bottom line of the hull.

KNOT

1. Something tied in a cord or rope.

2. 6,080 ft. per hour. A measure of velocity. One nautical mile per hour.

LAMINATING Laying layer upon layer.

LAMINATING RESIN A polyester resin with a thin, runny consistency, like a thin syrup.

LAY-UP The process of lamination.

LIFT

1. *Static*. What you get when a wave swells up under a canoe.

2. *Dynamic*. When a canoe is pushed along faster than its critical speed, it tries to lift out on to the surface of the water and starts to plane. This happens in surfing.

LONGITUDINAL Of or in the length of an object.

MASTER SECTION Look at the boat head on. Ignore the effect of perspective. One way to get rid of this effect is to look at a boat from a long way off, end on, using a telephoto lens of great power. The greatest girth of the boat is at its widest point, which is most usually in the middle or just aft of that point.

The shape of this section is a prime factor in deciding the whole shape of the boat, because once this shape has been given to the plans for the boat, the harmony of the lines of the boat dictates that shape should be reflected in every other section in the boat.

Therefore its name 'Master Section' is an apt one. The three basic shapes which could be used in hull design for the master section are a rectangle, a triangle, and a semi-circle. A square is stable, but has the greatest wetted area for a given buoyancy. The triangle is next, with a lesser wetted area, and hence less

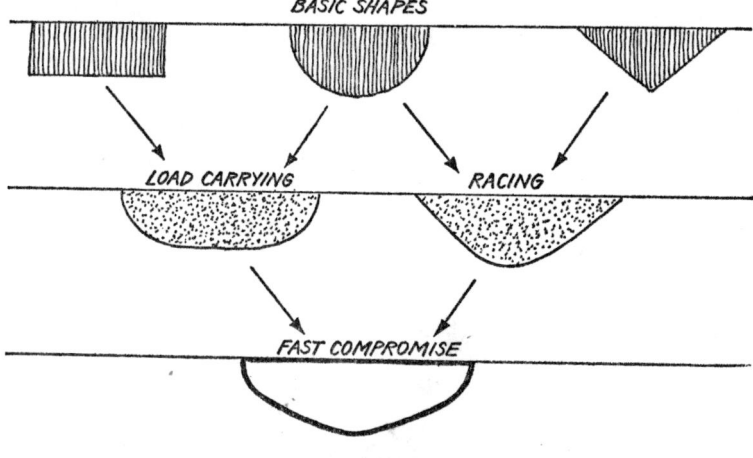

Fig. 65

skin drag. The semi-circle is best of all with a minimum wetted area and hence lowest skin drag. It is also the most difficult to balance.

In practice the sections are composites. The flat-bottomed shape with rounded bilges turning up into flat, vertical sides, gives the typical load-carrying barge-like hull. The eskimo kayak of the predominantly Greenland-type, is built with a keel, two bilges or chines, and two gunwales. It is a flattened triangle which widens out into a steep sided triangle. The reason for this is primarily lack of long timbers in Greenland.

Did you ever wonder why flat-bottomed boats seem to be so stable? You can go for a walk from side to side, almost, in some of the older canvas canoes, without seriously upsetting the trim of the boat. The boat always tries to conform with the water surface. If the surface of the water is flat, the boat will sit flat on it. If the water tilts, and even goes vertical, as it does just before a wave breaks, then the boat will go vertical, and there is nothing you can do about it.

On the other hand you may have entered a narrow slim kayak, and wobbled about most horribly on flat water, and thought 'This damn thing frightens me! How can anyone paddle this on rough water?' The answer is simple. Get used to it, then go away and find some rough water. (Remember a good basic rule for sea going. 'Less than three there should never be.') Then, when a wave sweeps up to you, and tries to turn you vertical, it cannot, because the hull has so little 'bite' on the water that the wave slips away underneath and doesn't affect your balance a fraction as much as it would a flat-bottomed boat.

Perhaps the boat you want is to turn easily. Give it lots of rocker, say 8 in. each end, and widen out the master section and give it a flat bottom. It has a fair bit of buoyancy at a shallow draught, so that the centre part of the hull carries most of the load. This leaves the ends free to turn above the water when possible, although still there to give lift in heavy water conditions.

A good sea boat typically has a slightly veed bottom, with rounded keel and rounded chines, with a slight flare up to the gunwales. It is a flattish sort of boat, sitting down on to the water, trying to get more bite in the sea than on the air above it. Its ends tend to be deep vees, with lots of 'dig' at the stern. The bow tends to rise up to a fair amount of rocker. The dig at the stern is to keep the centre of lateral pressure behind the centre of effort, so that the boat tends to trail and keep a straight track. It reduces turning ability.

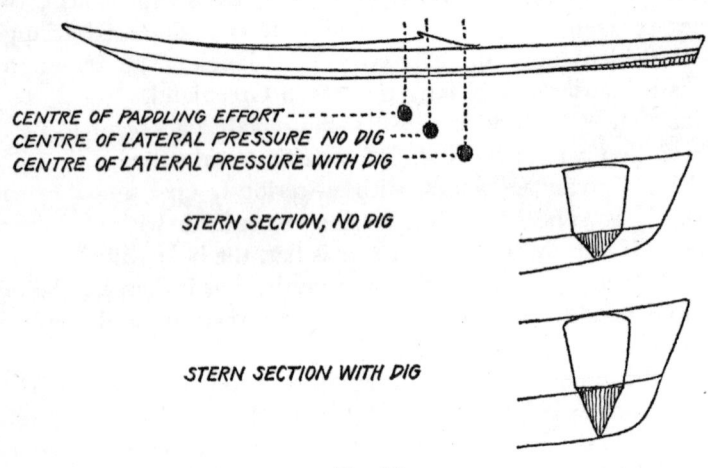

CENTRE OF PADDLING EFFORT ----------
CENTRE OF LATERAL PRESSURE NO DIG ----
CENTRE OF LATERAL PRESSURE WITH DIG ------

STERN SECTION, NO DIG

STERN SECTION WITH DIG

Fig. 66

A racing kayak (K1) plays one or two tricks, and can even become quite a freak, because of the restrictions that competition rules apply. There is a minimum beam specified. This is about 19 in. However, the minimum waterline beam could be as little as 16 in., and some reckon that skilled paddlers could paddle boats with a narrower beam than that. It would indeed be interesting to see what would happen if International Competition rules were relaxed on racing K1s. Nevertheless, since rules there are, they must be obeyed.

Now, if one must bring the beam out to a certain width, there is nothing to state that this must be done at the waterline. It must be the gunwale width. Suppose we give the waterline

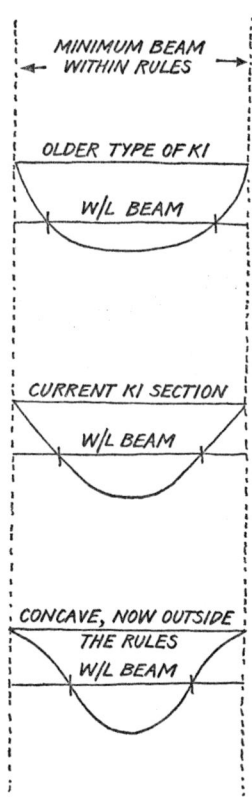

Fig. 67

beam a width of 16 in., and make the hull section up to that point a semi-circle almost. The sides at the waterline then spring away as tangents to that semi-circle. These sides then rise to the gunwale.

If the radius of the semi-circle is made too small, we land up with a triangular section with a rounded bottom, and so lose the benefit of minimum wetted area. If we make the semi-circle of too large a diameter it loses the benefit of narrow waterline beam. The factor which decides this is the weight of the load applied. The boat itself has a certain minimum weight according to rule, and the paddler's weight then varies. A certain racing craft will produce its best performance for a person of a certain weight. One lighter, or heavier, will not be getting the best out of the boat. The difference is small, maybe 0.1 per cent, but for an equal effort, that is 1 metre in a thousand metre sprint, quite enough to win or lose by. I do not design for competition, but those who do must know for whom they do design.

Maybe you have a bright idea, such as this. Why not design a slalom type of kayak, with lots of rocker, and so manouevrable, but give it a rounded vee bottom for speed as well? Best of both worlds? Not on your life.

What happens is this. Maybe you have a design waterline in mind, and in my case I work on a 4-in. waterline. You put lots of rocker into the profile, and then you make the master section slim. Well this means that for a given load, a

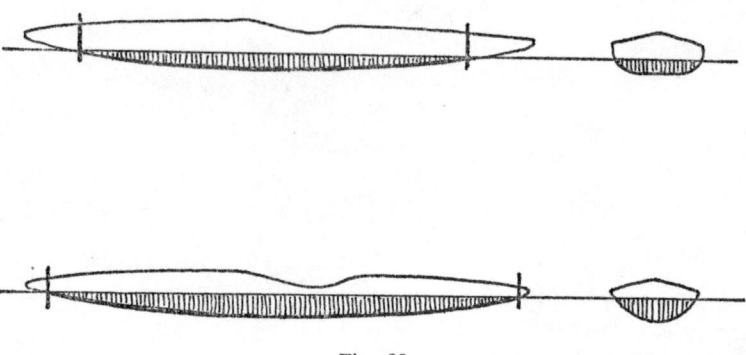

Fig. 68

slalom craft with a rounded flat-bottom will sit at its 4-in. draught, and the rockered ends will rise above the water. But if the centre section is reduced in bulk by giving it a rounded vee, the whole boat simply sits deeper into the water, and the effect of the highly rockered ends is lost. You now have a slow boat which won't turn.

Some years ago I designed a slalom boat, called the OX 1. Short for 'Oxford first design'. It was designed around three sets of lines cunningly traced from adverts in *Canoeing* for the Gaybo 'Funa', the Streamlyte 'KW7' and the Portable Boats 'Klepper SL 7'. These three sets of lines were magnified to one-tenth size, and then averaged out on to squared paper. I had to guess at the master section in each case. A photograph about $3\frac{1}{2}$ in. long doesn't reveal much! Like all things designed by committees, instead of being a horse it was a camel. Or so I thought at first. It had a lean entry, a moulding fault gave it a beam 2 in. less than the slalom rules permitted, and it didn't turn at all well, as my penchant for sea kayaks caused me to give it a rounded although flattened vee bottom. It was quite fast, and many enjoyed using it on the sea. I saw it once sitting in a stopper at the bottom of Iffley weir, sitting flat and even like a tram on rails. Typical slalom boats around it were being bounced about all over the place, and were giving their paddlers plenty to do. But the OX 1 sat there obviously at ease. Well, if you want a kayak that is happy in stoppers, I have designed one. I think that was the result of its lean entry giving the water less grip forward, and its flattened stern sliding over the water at the rear, more like a planing form suitable for surfing.

MEASURE

1. *Imperial.* The system of measurement deriving its authority from UK statute. This book is written with Imperial measure in mind, and often a mixture of Imperial and Metric measure is used, i.e., 7 ml. of catalyst to 1 lb. of resin. (ml. is one millilitre, lb. is one pound weight.)

2. *Metric.* All the European communities are going over, officially, to metric measure. I think in terms of Imperial still, and I fear I always will, and shall therefore be obliged to do a calculation to convert one to the other.

Conversion:

1 in.	=25. 4mm.
1 ft.	=304.8 mm.
1 sq. in.	=645.2 sq. mm.
1 sq. ft.	=0.09290 sq. m.
1 cu. in.	=16,387 cu. mm.
1 cu. ft.	=0.02832 cu. m.
1 lb.	=0.45 kg.

META CENTRE This term means the centre from which measurements are taken. Especially it means the centre from which
measurements of stability are taken. There are three meta centres
on a boat, one for lateral stability (rolling qualities), one for
longitudinal stability (yawing or turning qualities) and another
for pitching or looping qualities. That which is easiest to describe
and which has most use is that for lateral stability.

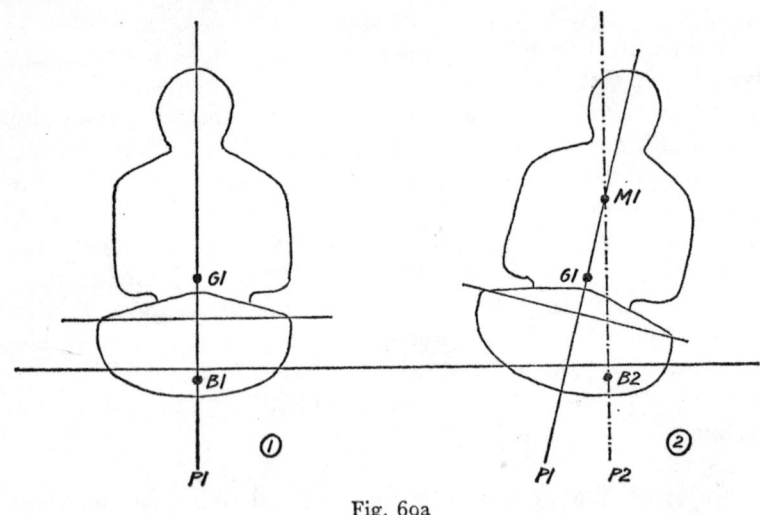

Fig. 69a

In the drawing, (1) the canoeist is sitting straight up, and not
moving. The canoe is on still flat water. It has a centre of
buoyancy, B1, and a centre of gravity of canoe and paddler,
G1. A vertical line P1 runs straight up right through both B1
and G1.

The canoe tilts over slightly. (2) The centre of buoyancy
moves across because the shape of the canoe under water has

changed. This new centre of buoyancy is B2. A new vertical through B2 is now P2 where the new vertical and the old intersect at M1, is the meta centre. The distance G1–M1 is a measure of the stability of the canoe and paddler. Anything which can be done to increase G1–M1 is an advantage in securing stability on still water. The easiest way is to make the canoe very wide. But if this is done, it becomes impossible to reach over the sides to paddle, and if it turns over no amount of skill will ever right it. So a compromise must be found.

Still keeping the shape of the canoe slim and rounded, one can shift the meta centre upwards quite a lot by moving the body. The third drawing shows how this works. The canoeist leans away from the tilt. This feels as if you were letting the canoe fall away into a worse tilt, in fact. An expert canoeist will be 'riding' the canoe in an easy way, allowing his hips to tilt with the canoe. If you try and hold the canoe level by hip action, you effectively worsen the condition that is leading to a loss of balance.

When the canoeist leans over, he shifts his centre of gravity from G1 to G2. For the sake of simplicity, I have shown the new vertical when in the level position, as being P1(a). It is parallel

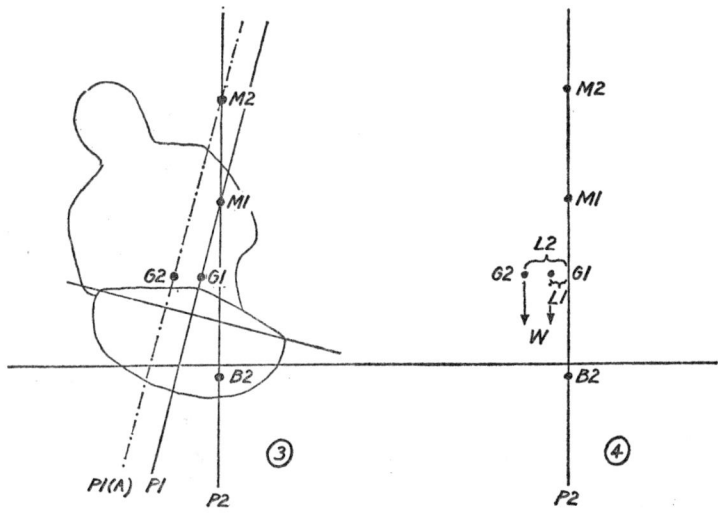

Fig. 69b

to P_1 and replaces P_1. This line when projected upward intersects the vertical in the tilted position, P_2, at M_2. This is the new meta centre. The measure of stability is now G_2-M_2, just about twice the righting moment of the first position.

The righting moment is represented by the perpendicular distance of the centre of gravity from the vertical, multiplied by the weight acting at the centre of gravity. The fourth drawing shows this effect. The distance of G_1 from the vertical P_1 is L_1, and the distance of G_2 from the vertical P_1 is L_2. In each case the weight, let it be W, is the same. So that the greater righting effect when you lean away from the tilt is represented by the proportion $L_2 : L_1$.

What can one deduce from all this? Well, a small agile person is likely to do better in rough water than a big rangy one, although the big fellow can apply his effort more powerfully to the water and is likely to make a better sprinter, for example. A person who has a big powerful chest and heavy head will be less stable than a person who has heavy legs and a lightweight head. The person who is willing to lean as described will be on better balance than one who is not. Learning to relax is a large part of skill in anything. The expert anything always makes it look as if he had time in hand for anything he does. In design you can move the meta centre further from the centre of gravity by making the boat wider, or giving it a flatter bottom for a given beam, or even by playing around with concave cross sections, rather like a catamaran. But then you will pay a penalty in increased wetted area, and freakish reactions to ordinary handling techniques.

MOMENTS The product of weight and leverage (in this case). Two people sit on a see-saw. One is a man of 12 st., one is a boy of 6 st. To keep the balance, the man must sit closer to the pivot point. He must sit at exactly half the distance from the pivot compared with the distance at which the boy must sit. Their moments are the same.

MOULD Either male or female. Male moulds are polished on the outside, female moulds are polished on the inside. Hull and deck moulds are female, cockpit moulds are male. The grp laminate is laid up on the polished surface.

OFFSETS At each station on the datum line, any point on the periphery of the section shape can be placed by two offsets, or ordinates, one vertical and one horizontal, all measured at right angles to the datum line.

PLAN What you see from directly above the object.

PLANING Going fast enough to ride on the surface of the water. About 8 to 10 knots for an ordinary canoe.

PLASTICENE A proprietary brand of modelling clay, very useful for mould correction or small details. Re-useable.

PSI Pounds per sq. in. A measure (Imperial) of pressure. 1 atmosphere is 14.7 psi. Also the head of water in feet multiplied by 0.43=psi.

PVA Poly-vinyl-alcohol. A release agent soluble in alcohol or water. It is impervious to resin when dry. It makes a good release agent for quick mouldings where surface finish is not very important. It tends to leave brush marks on the finished laminate.

PLUG The first shape from which the moulds are made. Has a highly polished surface. Can be called the pattern.

PRISMATIC CO-EFFICIENT A figure less than one. Relates the volume of the immersed part of the hull to the volume of a rectangular block which has three dimensions, these being the length waterline, beam waterline, and draught. A flat-bottomed barge will have a PC nearer to one than a round-bottomed racing craft. Designers try to get a pc of less than 0.5 for racing craft.

PROFILE What you see when you look at the side view of an object.

RAIL A surfboard term being the edge where the planing bottom of the board turns up to the side. A hard rail has a radius of about $\frac{1}{8}$-in., a soft rail a radius of upwards of $\frac{1}{2}$-in. Hard rails give speed, soft rails manoeuvrability.

RAKE The line of the stem of the boat as it rises up from waterline to the point of the bow. A kayak has a typically high raking bow. Gives a springing ride in head waves for much the same reason as a flared bow. Flare and rake are linked together.

ROCKER The degree of curvature in a vertical plane of the keel line. With the centre of the canoe on the ground, the ends rise up towards the bow or stern. The degree of rise is called the rocker. Downturned ends, called negative rocker are almost always a design or construction fault.

SEAT BRACE Fixed between the side of the seat and the inside of the hull. It stops the seat swaying sideways. If the seat sways it gives a feeling of instability, and eventually causes early laminate failure and separation of the seat bottom from the seat sides.

SECTION What you see from directly in front of or behind an object. At the widest point it is called the master section.

SHEER The upward curve of the gunwale when seen in profile, from the middle towards the ends. This is positive sheer and is frequently a quality of beautiful sailing clippers and sea-going kayaks. Negative sheer is seen most often in power boats where the impression desired is one of brute power, a decision to ignore the usual dictates of the sea and nature. Many river canoes or kayaks have no sheer, being neutral.

SHIP Strictly a three-masted ship with square rig on all three masts. This distinguishes it from a barque which is only fore and aft rigged on the third mast.

SKEG a fixed rudder. It effectively brings the centre of lateral pressure more towards the stern, and helps to make the craft stiff directionally.

SKIN DRAG Same as drag. (qv.)

SPECIFIC WEIGHT Take a sheet of glass mat. I would call it $1\frac{1}{2}$-oz. mat. Others would call it 450 g. per sq. m., $1\frac{1}{2}$ oz. is what one sq. ft. of it weighs. A laminate composed of 2 layers of $1\frac{1}{2}$-oz. mat is called a 3-oz. laminate, and the weight of the resin is ignored. Woven rovings, or cloth as it sometimes called (erroneously) is measured in ounces per square yard or grams per square metre. 9-oz. 'cloth' has the same specific weight as 1-oz. mat.

SPINE There are several ways of building a canoe, or a plug. From the keel upwards, or from the gunwale frame both upwards and downwards, or from a central spine running longitudinally from bow to stern. (*See* plug construction)

SPRAY DECK It must stand up to more than spray. It is simply a flexible seal between the paddler's body and the rim of the cockpit. It must be easily removable in difficulties so that the canoeist can get out. It must have a release strap or becket.

STABILITY Stay-ability. In a boat it is measured in three ways, lateral S., directional S., and pitching or looping S. This is the order in which one first experiences them. Most novices are most sensitive to lateral S. Progress is marked next by the ability to overcome directional *in*stability.

STATION The points along the datum line where the sections are to be put.

STERN Back end of boat. Corruption of 'steering end'.

STIFF A resistance the boat has to any change of attitude, it can be stiff in rolling (i.e. flat-bottomed, wide) or stiff to turn (i.e. vee bottomed, lots of dig at stern, or with skeg attached) or stiff to loop (i.e. a long boat, or a short surfing boat with very 'turned-up' ends).

STOPPER A term used in the sport of white water canoeing. This is typically a standing wave which is found just behind a covered rock over which the water flows very fast and in great volume. The standing wave curls back, and to enter this wave at speed is to feel a sensation just like slamming on the brakes of a fast car very hard. To go into it slowly is asking to be turned end over end and held in the stopper. This is very dangerous.

STRINGER A longitudinal structural member, usually $\frac{3}{4}$-in. by $\frac{1}{2}$-in. in canoe construction.

SURF SHOE A special canoe for surfing, short, say 10 ft., with a sudden high raked bow to prevent pearl-diving or digging-in of the bow. The line of maximum beam is below the water-line. It is a planing boat.

SURFSKI A special form of long surfboard, used in surf rescue, paddled with double-ended kayak paddles. These are used in competition, being solo or double. A special solo rescue ski is now in use in South Africa and Australia which is short say 10 ft., beam about 32 in., and bulky, being buoyant enough to support two people in surf. It has a surfboard bottom like a Malibu board.

TRANSOM A square-ended stern. Unusual in canoes or kayaks. Grumman aluminum Canadian canoes are built this way to take the clamps of outboards. The NCK 1 and NCK 2 were used in competition in Great Britain in the late fifties and early sixties, and they had transom sterns.

TRANSVERSE Of or in the width of an object, at right angles to the longitudinal.

TUMBLEHOME Seen in section. The upper part of the hull is narrower than at the waterline. Often seen in the stern shape of speedboats. Typical of the Micmac canoe of Eastern Canada.

VERTICAL ACCELERATION An object floats in the water. A wave advances and the object rises with it. When an object changes its position it must be accelerated, in this case vertically upwards. The possible rate of acceleration is produced by the excess of buoyancy over weight. The rate of acceleration to stay afloat is demanded by the steepness of the wave face and the speed at which it passes.

WATERLINE In plan it outlines the surface area of the water which the hull displaces.

WATERPLANE The horizontal slice of the hull at any given draught, outlined by the waterline at that draught.

WAVE CURRENT There are two in each wave that affect the canoeist by affecting the ends of the canoe, thus affecting the steering. In the trough there is a movement towards the next crest, contrary to the general wave movement. In the crest there is an enhanced movement in the direction of the wave movement.

WAX BUILD-UP When a mould has been polished too much, in that too much wax has been rubbed on to it without it being properly buffed up, then the wax begins to accrete into a gritty surface like fine sand. The mould must then be cut back with cutting paste.

WEATHERCOCK As a weathercock points into the wind, so will a badly balanced kayak swing bows to wind on the sea. A common fault with river craft in strong cross winds.

WETTED SURFACE Total area of the immersed surface of the hull.

WETTING OUT When the glass had been wetted through with resin, and the resin has softened the binder on the glass, entrapped air bubbles are seen and are removed by rolling. The resulting laminate is then wetted out.

WETTING THROUGH This comes before wetting out. The mould has resin in it, and the glass is pressed down into it. The resin rises up through the glass strands and as the colour of the resin stains the white of the glass, it is wetting through.

WINDAGE If a floating object is only just buoyant it will ride low in the water. The wind cannot much affect it. If the object is very buoyant then it will ride high and the wind can catch and move it. This effect is called windage.

Bibliography

The Bark Canoes and the Skin Boats of North America. E. T. Adney and H. I. Chapelle. Smithsonian Institute, Washington DC. 1964.

This is a source book, I would say *the* source book for canoe and kayak design. If you want to know about what the Indians built, and how they built it, this book will tell you. In it there are many line drawings quite detailed enough to allow full size working drawings to be developed from them. The eskimo kayaks are from both shores of the North American continent, and from Baffin Bay.

Skene's Elements of Yacht Design, revised by Francis S. Kinney, A. & C. Black, 1962.

It is about yacht design, but there are many parts of it which are more general in their approach, and which would help an earnest student to acquire greater knowledge of the principles involved in small hull design. It has a considerable amount of mathematics in it.

Sailing Theory and Practice. C. A. Marchaj. Adlard Coles, 1971.

This book is full of beautiful drawings, dealing again with sailing yachts, the design of hulls and sails, and the influence on airflow of masts, and so on. It also has a section on the design features of the International 10 sq. m. sailing canoe, which is round about the size we are interested in. It has many photographs which are good to look at. Not a source of information for canoe builders, unless they want to study the subject of design in a wider way.

Rushton and His Times in American Canoeing. Atwood Manley. Adirondack Museum, 1968.

Traces the history of American sporting canoeing from the eighteen-sixties. It has several line drawings of some very good wooden-built 'Canadian' canoes, of the type which are still to be seen for hire on the Thames at Oxford, or on the Wear at Durham. Given the photographs too, it would be possible to build such a canoe in the old way.

Canoes and Canoeing. Percy Blandford. Lutterworth, 1962.

This is all about canvas canoe types and construction. It was on these types that I had my introduction to canoeing in 1957. The book has small sketches from which one could develop full size working drawings. Percy Blandford writes many books on canoeing and small boats.

British Coracles and Irish Curraghs. James Hornell. National Maritime Museum Greenwich, first published 1936–37–38.

Papers still available. This is *the* source book on the native British small boats. Has many small but accurately detailed drawings of curraghs and coracles.

Surf and Sea. John M. Kelly Jr. Barnes, New York, 1965.

Full of photographs and the history of surfing. In particular it has two chapters on the criteria affecting surfboard design, and is the only work on planing surfboard design that I have seen. You could design you own board from this. However, it is 'old fashioned' in the surfing sense, as now people are using very small, short boards which quite put the old Malibu boards in the shade.

Canoeing Complete. Edited by Brian Skilling. Kaye-Ward, 1973.

Chapter 9 is on canoe design, and is by Jorgen Samson, a Dane, who designs racing kayaks. In it also is a chapter on canoe construction which gives some idea of the outline of canoe building.

Practical Ship Stability. Captain K. Macdonald. Brown Son and Ferguson, 1946.

Some one gave me this slim little book years ago. It is written for Merchant Navy Deck Officers, and deals with GM measurements for small cargo vessels. This is where I first read of the meta-centre. Nothing for the canoeist apart from the principles involved, and interesting in its own right.

The magazine *Canoeing,* if you can find a full set from December 1959, has many articles which bear on design and construction. I have a full set, but now I do not lend them out. Address 25 Featherbed Lane Croydon, CRO 9AE. The magazine *Canoeing in Britain* is also useful in this way. Address 70 Brompton Road London SW3 1 Dt.

Living Canoeing. Alan Byde. A. & C. Black, 1969.
Mostly on the handling of canoes, with a little (rather old-fashioned) on canoe construction. Good background reading.

Beginner's Guide to Canoeing. Alan Byde. Pelham, 1974.
Its been called 'One Man's View of Canoeing' and that by several who know me well. Not much on canoe design or construction, but interesting. Don't take my word for it, read it.

Canoe Building. Alan Byde. A. & C. Black, 1974.
There are many differences between this book and the book in which you are reading about it. If you were to put them together and read through one and then the other, you would have most of the knowledge I have been able to gain about canoe design and construction in the last eighteen years. Call these two books complementary.

Finally, a note for historical reasons. Dick Gayes, of Leicester, wrote a paper on canoe design methods, and it is first class. It puts forward a sophisticated geometrical method which I've never used, but I have seen it used. Once the essential dimensions and the master section have been chosen, you apply the method and out pops the drawing like sausages from a machine. Dick dropped out of canoeing in a dramatic way, he swapped his kayak for a parachute.

APPENDIX ONE

Fail-safe Footrest

Frank Goodman who helped to criticise this book designed the fail-safe footrest. His description follows. I think it is very well worth while including it. Matters which affect life cannot ever be ignored, and so this aspect is getting especial notice in this book.

The failsafe Footrest described on page 119 was the first failsafe device that was simple, inexpensive, and didn't add weight to the canoe. However, while it certainly prevented the canoeist's feet from jamming, it unfortunately took away some of the strength of the canoe; insomuch that it did not hold the two gunwales together, as did the simple bar footrests that had bolts at each end, fastening into a horizontal plate.

This can be a serious defect, because a canoe forced beneath the surface during a surfing spree, or during the negotiation of heavy rapids, can have very severe pressures put upon it. These forces tend to crush in the deck and hull and at the same time spread the gunwales apart. In extreme conditions the pressure will rupture the deck, and force the gunwale so far apart that the deck collapses on to the feet – almost as bad as jamming behind the footrest.

It became clear that a fail-safe footrest that not only swung clear of jammed feet, but also held the gunwales together would give the very best possible answer. But was it possible? Valley Canoe Products spent some considerable effort in their search for a perfect footrest, and eventually came up with their Tie-Beam Fail-Safe footrest. TBFS for short.

As its name implies it fails safe, and also forms a tie beam from gunwale to gunwale in the in-use position. The TBFS is protected by patent, but Valley Canoe Products feels that it should be freely available, as it has already been instrumental in saving at least two lives. The locking clips are already being supplied to many other canoe manufacturers throughout the world. The clips and the complete footrest are available to the amateur builder who wishes to incorporate the TBFS into canoes built by himself.

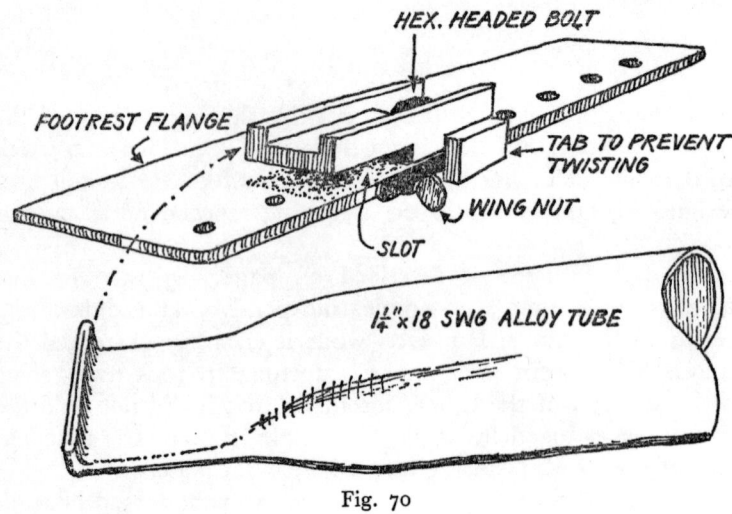

Fig. 70

APPENDIX TWO

British Canoe Union list of Canoe Manufacturers and Materials Suppliers

Suppliers Code
A   Manufacturers and Agents of Rigid Canoes
B   Manufacturers and Agents of Folding Canoes
C   Manufacturers and Agents of Sailing Canoes
D   Manufacturers and Agents of Canadian Canoes
E   DIY Canoe Kit Suppliers
F   Canoe Plans Suppliers
G   Glass Fibre Moulds, Suppliers and Hirers
H   Canoe Hirers
I   Canoe Accessories including Paddles
J   Canoe Accessories excluding Paddles
K   Canoe Trailers and Couplings
L   Lifejackets and Clothing
M   Suppliers of Glassfibre material
N   Suppliers of Roof Racks
*Slalom   only.   **Canadian   Only.
***Crash Helmets and Paddles.

SUPPLIER	CODE
AC Canoe Products (Chester) Ltd., 5 Walnut Close, Upton-by-Chester. Tel: Chester 25277.	I***
Aquaquipment, 4 Ashwell Street, St Albans, Herts. Tel: 66666.	J
Ashford Marine (J. L. Gmach) Ltd., Ashford Works, 9 Ashford Road Fordingbridge, Hants. Tel: Fordingbridge 2422.	A

SUPPLIER	CODE
Avoncraft, Burrowfield, Welwyn Garden City, Herts. Tel: 07073 3000.	A,D,E,G,I,K,L
P. W. Blandford, Quinton House, Newbold-on-Stour, Stratford-on-Avon, Warwickshire. CV37 24A. Tel: Alderminster 257.	F
Canoe Centre, Marsh Lane, Crediton, Devon. Tel: 3295. 18 Beauchamp Road, Twickenham, Middlesex. Tel: 8979.	A,B,D,I.K.L
Captain Frank McNulty & Sons Ltd., Victoria Road, South Shields, Co. Durham. Tel: South Shields 63196.	A,G,I,L
The Wild Water Centre, The Mill, Glasshouses, Pateley Bridge, Harrogate, North Yorks. HG3 5QH. Tel: Pateley Bridge 624 and 310 Chrisfilms – address as above.	A,E,G,I,K, Canoeing Films L,M
C. P. Witter Ltd., Chester CH1 3LL. †Also Trailer Touring Brackets. Tel: 0244 4116.	*K
Cymru Canoes (GB) Ltd., St Hilary's Road, Llandudno LL30 1PU Tel: 0492 77067.	A
D. J. Davis (DK Designs) 12 Cecil Park, Herne Bay, Kent. CT6 6Dl. 0227-375729	F
Euro Kayaks, 13 Ravine Road, Canford Cliffs, Poole Dorset BH13 7HS. Tel: 0202 709792.	A,L,K,L,N
FI.BO Wolverhampton Ltd., 72 Billy Bunn's Lane, Wombourne, Wolverhampton.	A
Gaybo Ltd., 4 Rose Hill, Brighton, Sussex DN2 3FA. Tel: 684599.	A,D,I,L

SUPPLIER	CODE
Mark Gees, 61 Thames Eyot, Cross Deep, Twickenham, TW1 4QL. Tel: 01-892 3635.	I (paddles only)
Granta Boats Ltd., Ramsey, Huntingdon PE17 1HG. Tel: Ramsey Hunts 3777.	A,B,C,D,E,F,G, H,I,J,K,L,N
Granta Canoes, 640 High Road, N. Finchley, London, N12. Tel 01-445 Tel: 01-445 9933.	
Harishok Ltd., Unit 3, Clarendon Trading Estate, Clarendon Road, Hyde, Cheshire SK14 2LJ. Tel: 061-368 9216.	L
G. G. & M. E. Hinton, Milton Street, Fairford, Gloucs. Tel: Fairford 540.	A,D,E,F,I,L
Howarth Sports, 27 Limefield Road, Smithills, Bolton, Lancs. Tel: 4377.	L
Jon Hyland, 42 Diddington Lane, Hampton in Arden, Solihull, Warks. B92 0BZ. Tel: (067 55) 2247.	A,G,I
Jaycee Glassfibre Products, 69 Knights Hill, West Norwood, London, SE 27. Tel: 01-670 1234.	A,I
Jenkins & Lancefield, 'Moonraker' Canoes, Corsham, Wilts. Tel: Corsham 713346.	
Canoe & Outdoor Activity Centre, Lake Farm, Carlton Miniott, Thirsk, Yorks. Tel: Thirsk 23106.	A,E,I,L
Joseph Bank Ltd., 749 Knutsford Road, Latchford Village, Warrington. Tel: Warrington 31569.	A,I,L
J. & J. Kirkham, 9–11, Hr. Church Street, Blackburn, Lancs. Tel: Blackburn 57688.	A,I,L

SUPPLIER	CODE
Lendal of Scotland (Wilson (Prest-wick) Ltd.,) 18–20 Boyd Street, Prestwick, Ayrshire, Scotland. Tel: (0292) 78558) KA9 1LG.	E,F,I,L
Vic Lewis Boats, 12 Henshaw Road, Small Heath, Birmingham 10.	A,D,E,I,K,L
Mountain Centre, 34 Dean Street, Newcastle-upon-Tyne. Tel: 23561.	L
Mountain Craft Ltd., 9 Hammerton Street, Burnley, Lancs. Tel: Burnley 38470.	A,I,L
Ottersports, Ash Street, Northampton. Tel: 39405 and 39161.	A,D,E,I,L
P & H Fibreglass Products, 76 Dale Road, Spondon, Derby. Tel: Ilkeston 3155 and Derby 61108.	A,D,E,G,I,K,L
P.G.L. Adventure Ltd., 32–34 Station Street, Ross-on-Wye, Herefordshire. Tel: Ross (0989)4211.	H
Pyranha Mouldings Ltd., 53 Poachers Lane, Latchford, Warrington, Cheshire. WA4 1TP. Tel: Warrington 31484.	A
*Strand Glass Co. Lt*d., 109 High Street, Brentford, Middlesex and Branches. Tel: 01-568 7191.	E,G,M
Streamlyte Canoes, 206 Amyand Park Road, St Margarets, Twickenham, Middlesex.	A,G,I,K,L
Topcraft Ltd., 324a, Birmingham Road, Walsall. Tel: 0922 28329.	A
Traykin Ltd., Station House, Postland, Crowland, Peterborough, Tel: Whaplode Drove 408.	A,I

SUPPLIER	CODE
Trylon Ltd., Thrift Street, Wollaston, Northants NH9 7QJ. Also canoe technical service and free technical literature, Canoe Building Demonstrations, Canoe Building Booklets for glassfibre canoes. Tel: 093 363 275.	E,F,G,I,L,N
Tyne Canoes Ltd., 206 Amyand Park Road, St. Margarets, Twickenham, Middlesex. Tel: 01-892 4033.	A,B,C,D,E,F,G,I, K,L
Valley Canoe Products, Ltd., Private Road, 4, Colwick Estate, Nottingham. Tel: 0602 249271.	A,E,G,H,I,K,L
Watling Works, 88 Parkstreet Village, St Albans, Herts. Also canoe carriers and roof racks for cars and vans. Tel: 0727 73661.	K
Wyvern Boats (Wessex) Ltd., Park Street, Yeovil, Somerset. Tel: Yeovil	EI,L

APPENDIX THREE

Constructional Standards

There are two bodies which set standards of canoe construction in Britain. These are :

The British Canoe Manufacturers Association
R. H. Goodman
58 Loughborough Road
Bunny
Notts

The British Standards Institution
2 Park Street
London WIA 2Bs.

At the time of writing the BSI has not yet established its recommendations. You may obtain the regulations from the address given.

The BCMA recommendations are as follows. *Standards of Construction and Safety.* (Amended November 1973)

The standards apply to closed cockpit canoes where in the paddling position the legs of the canoeist are covered by the structure of the canoe. Standards B10, B11, and B12 need not be applied to open cockpit canoes, where in the normal paddling position the legs of the canoeist are not enclosed by the structure of the canoe. There is an exemption, which applies to Baths Training or play canoes designed specifically for use on calm waters; canoes sold in kit form or part finished, where the manufacturer has no control over the finished product, or any canoe made from materials other than reinforced plastics. Sometimes the customer may specify a canoe for his personal use which does not meet the standards of the Association. In that case the boat will be clearly marked 'To Customer Specification'.

STANDARDS. PART A. CONSTRUCTION.

A1 All polyester resins must be of the type specified by the resin manufacturers as being suitable for marine usage.

A2 All reinforcing materials must be of a type specified by the reinforcement manufacturer as being suitable for marine useage.

A3 All organic peroxide hardeners, accelerators and pigments must be compatible with the types of resin used.

A4 All reinforcements must be properly 'wetted-out', well consolidated and free from trapped air.

A5 The gel, or surface coating, shall be free from obvious blemish, wrinkling, blistering, and colour streaking.

A6 The interior of the laminate shall be smooth and the seating area shall be free of all rough patches, sharp edges, and projections.

A7 The seat and cockpit must be of stronger construction than the surrounding areas.

A8 Joins between separately laminated mouldings of the same structure must be non-porous and be reinforced with similar materials to those used in the main structure.

A9 Where polyester reinforcement is used as a complete laminate in the hull moulding, the same laminate must not be used in the deck moulding.

PART B (SAFETY)

B1 Provision must be made for the fitting of end loops and/or toggles.

B2 Where fitted, toggles must be securely fixed with rot-proof line and must withstand a stress of not less than 200 Kg. applied between the toggle and the canoe. Toggles shall measure not less than 75 mm. in length and 20 mm. in diameter.

B3 Where fitted, painter lines must be secured in such a way as to hold them away from the cockpit area.

B4 Each canoe must be fitted with at least 25 kg. of positive buoyancy so placed that, when full of water, the canoe will float in a normal horizontal position and will support a weight of $12\frac{1}{2}$ kg. placed at either end of the canoe, or at both ends simultaneously.

B5   Solid expanded foam buoyancy must be of the closed cell type with a maximum 1 per cent vol/vol absorption rate. (Standard test: 6-in. cube, 48-in. head, 14 day immersion, all cut surfaces.)

B6   Pillar buoyancy must be securely fixed so as not to become free when the canoe is waterlogged. It should be placed to add to the structural strength of the canoe.

B7   Water exclusion buoyancy of the sealed bulkhead type must not be used unless (a) sufficient closed cell foam is enclosed to standard B4, and (b) drainage plugs or caps are fitted to the bulkhead to allow easy removal of any water seepage.

B8   Air Bag buoyancy must have provision on the bags to allow them to be tied into position so that a partially deflated bag cannot float out of a capsized canoe.

B9   All footrests shall be made of materials which can be shown not to deteriorate under the conditions of service.

B10 All footrest assemblies shall be able to stand without sign of damage a static load of at least 150 kg. placed at a single central position and applied in the same direction as normal foot pressure.

B11 Platform-type footrests shall not, in any position, permit the canoeists feet to pass forward of the nootrest. It shall be rigidly fixed and incapable of rotation on its mountings.

B12 Bar type footrests must be so designed to allow the canoeist to remove his feet or legs, should they pass forward of the bar.

B13 Spray-covers when provided must be fitted with a release becket or strap to enable the canoeist to remove the spray cover from the cockpit rim. The spraycover shall also enable the canoeist to leave the canoe in an emergency without the use of the release becket or strap.

APPENDIX FOUR

Competition Class Restrictions (Construction)

Type	Max length	Min length	Max beam	Min beam	Min weight
SLALOM					
K1		4.00 m.		0.60 m.	
C1		4.00 m.		0.70 m.	
C2		4.58 m.		0.80 m.	
SPRINT					
K1	5.20 m.			0.51 m.	12 kg.
K2	6.50 m.			0.55 m.	18 kg.
K4	11.00 m.			0.60 m.	30 kg.
C1	5.20 m.			0.75 m.	16 kg.
C2	6.50 m.			0.75 m.	20 kg.
C7	11.00 m.			0.85 m.	50 kg.
POLO					
P1	3.00 m.	2.00 m.	0.60 m.	0.50 m.	

Note Roundness of ends not less than 50 mm. in radius in profile
Note Roundness of ends not less than 100 mm. in radius in plan

Type	Max length	Min length	Max beam	Min beam	Min weight
LONG DISTANCE RACING					
K1	5.20 m.			0.51 m.	12 kg.
K2	6.50 m.			0.55 m.	18 kg.
Class 3 (solo)	15 ft.			23 in.	
Class 4 (double)	18 ft.			24 in. (gunwale) 21 in. (waterline)	
Espada	One design K1				

Note Max length shall exclude rudder except where rudder is more than 1 in. thick at loaded waterline.
Transverse and longitudinal sections shall be convex and uninterrupted.
Class 4. Gunwale and waterline to be measured within 18 in. of mid point. Waterline beam measured at 4-in. draft.
Class 4. Distance between front of front seat and front of rear seat at maximum distance apart shall not exceed 6 ft.

Index